A Guide to...
Australian Long and Broad-tailed Parrots and New Zealand Kakarikis

By Kevin Wilson

Crimson-winged Parrot; Princess Parrot; Regent Parrot; Superb Parrot; King Parrot; Red-capped Parrot.; Mallee Ringnecked Parrot; Cloncurry Parrot; Port Lincoln Parrot; Twenty-eight Parrot; Red-fronted Kakariki and Yellow-fronted Kakariki.

Published and Edited by Australian Birdkeeper ©

Contents

**First Published 1990 by
Australian Birdkeeper
PO Box 6288,
South Tweed Heads,
NSW. 2486. Australia.
First Reprint 1992**

ISBN 0 9587455 3 6

Front Cover:
Top left: Princess Parrot cock
Btm Left: Red-capped Parrot cock
Btm Centre: Yellow-fronted Kakarikis
Btm Right: Australian King Parrot cock
Back Cover:
Twenty-eight Parrot
All cover photographs by Kevin Wilson

Design, Type and Art: Jackson Studios (Gold Coast)
Colour Separations: Haighs Foto Art (Brisbane)
Printing: Prestige Litho (Brisbane)

Acknowledgements

The author and the publisher would like to thank the following people for their assistance in the preparation of this book.
Dr Robert Marshall
Steve Sharp
Peter Odekerkin
Keith Gallagher
Ian Ward
Barry Hibbard
Des Spittal/Currumbin Sanctuary

About the Author

Kevin Wilson was born in London, UK where he kept Finches and Budgerigars as a young boy.

Living within cooee of London Zoo he could be found at the bird house almost weekly.

Kevin emigrated to the 'Land of Parrots' when seventeen and has since wallowed in the variety of Australian birds available to the aviculturist.

His love and interest in birds grew during three and a half years at Sydney's Taronga Zoo, followed by five and a half years in the pet and aviary bird industry.

Through these years photography has also been a passion and this, with his love for birds have fused well, particularly evident is this in his parrot articles for Australian Birdkeeper magazine and several books that have featured his work in its entirety.

His own collection of birds embraces mostly parrots and he has spent the last decade concentrating on breeding rare Australian and Foreign species.

Introduction

KEVIN WILSON

Introduction

Australian parrots have been a favourite with aviculturists around the world since the early nineteenth century and they still remain a firm favourite in the twentieth. In spite of this popularity, up until the last ten years or so, we have had very little knowledge about their proper care, their nutritional requirements and some of the secrets of breeding them successfully in aviculture. Never has this hobby been so important to our feathered friends as it is today.

With the natural habitat of some of these birds diminishing, it behoves every serious-minded aviculturist and newcomer to bird keeping to build up an accurate knowledge of these magnificent birds, as sadly, one day we may no longer have them with us, except in our aviaries. While mankind continues to recklessly plunder the earth and take and destroy the homes of our fellow creatures, we have to keep firmly in mind that these birds we are now breeding, may eventually be the foundation stock of re-introduced birds to the wild.

Even birds that seem apparently abundant today, may in just a few short years become dangerously threatened. Therefore, we all need to do our utmost, even though we may only have one or two pairs in our charge, in caring and breeding birds of all kinds. It is certainly a challenge for the newcomer just to breed them and for the experienced aviculturist to become unselfish enough to share what beneficial knowledge he or she may have with those others willing to learn.

General Management

Managing birds is probably more a case of applying common sense than anything else, as far as their immediate environment is concerned. A food or water dish placed under a perch allowing faeces to foul it, uneaten food left to rot and breed harmful bacteria or perhaps a small piece of wire protruding just far enough to catch in the leg band of your favourite bird are all common mistakes made by bird fanciers the world over. Yet they are mistakes that should never happen and by scrutinising your management programme, accidents and problems like these should be few and far between.

Of the species dealt with in this book, arguably only the Kakarikis should be housed in aviaries any smaller than 4m(12ft 4in) in length, 1m (3ft 4in) wide and 2m (6ft 8in) high. Healthy birds will live longer and breed more successfully. Their immediate environment is one of the single most contributing factors to the aforementioned. Consideration to its size, construction, furnishings and cleanliness are therefore all exceedingly important to any serious aviculturist.

Most Australian parrots are strong flyers and need to exercise not only their physical aspects to the full but also their mental attributes. This can hardly be done in a home where the proverbial "cat" cannot be swung. The world renowned aviculturist, the late Duke of Bedford, was convinced that birds kept in small areas eventually became "weakly" and any young if produced at all, were also of this disposition, leading eventually, he believed, to a strain of enervated birds. Far fetched one may suppose, but, at the least it would have to be true regarding their mental outlook.

Optimum health for your birds can be maintained by having a regular cleaning programme. This is just as important as regular feeding or regular de-worming. Some birds make more mess than others, with little consideration to where their droppings may end up. Weekly cleaning with disinfectant of any fouled perches, seed trays etc. is necessary to avoid the risk of disease. Some birds, particularly Princess Parrots, even though they may have an abundance of suitable perches throughout the aviary, usually choose to sit on the edge of the water dish, fouling it continually, something that, if allowed to continue over a period of time, could lead to disastrous results. One particular way that I have found to avoid this problem is to use half round (D shaped) water containers that are made from either plastic or metal and have two hooks. They should be no more than 10cm. across and should be hooked on the wire right in a corner at a convenient level for the birds to drink from. Because the container is not too large and unless their tails were to be pressed upwards and firmly against the corner wire, they cannot get their vents over the water. Even if not becoming spoiled by faeces, all water, seed and other food dishes need to be cleaned and disinfected on a regular scale. The floor of your aviary is no less important to keep scrupulously clean. The floor contains more germs that can be detrimental to your birds than any other single area. Concrete floors can be swept, scrubbed, hosed, and disinfected with relative ease. When laying a concrete floor, make certain that it is on a slight slope and has a drainage trench which will run off all rain water. If it collects in pools your birds will be constantly drinking water that has been fouled by their own droppings.

Dirt floors, while sometimes more attractive to native birds, as most do love to peck and scratch around, are obviously much more difficult to keep clean and parasite free. Apart from Kakarikis, who love to tear up any inkling of anything growing, no matter how large their aviary, Australian parrots will usually allow a measure of grass to grow on the floor of a dirt aviary. They can benefit from this especially when it goes to seed as well as looking a little more desirable than just "dirt." Care must be taken though when young birds are fledging, if they land or walk through long, wet grass late in the day, they may not "dry out" before they roost, consequently catching a chill.

An extremely useful and hygienic design for the control, particularly of worms is the suspended aviary. Its origin is attributed to Florida breeder, Ramon Noegel and are often referred to as Noegel cages. His cages are individual units made of welded mesh that stand some 90cm (3ft) from the ground. The width and height are also about 90cm (3ft) and length varies depending on the species housed, up to 3.5m (11ft 8in). Part of the aviary is covered with sheets of plastic for protection from the sun. In Australia, with such varied climates, a little more protection would be needed, especially from the wind. Nest boxes are hung on the outside allowing easy access for inspection. If birds need to be caught they can be done so fairly readily by inserting a partition part way along the cage and using a net attached to a long handle. The heralded benefit of such cages is that, because the occupants have no access to the ground and little or no access to their own faeces, they are not prone to the problems caused by intestinal worms. The popularity of suspended cages in the United States is immense while its acceptance in Australia has been a little more guarded.

Nevertheless, some experimentally minded aviculturists have begun using them in a variety of modified ways. While there has been successful breedings with most species housed in this manner, it remains to be seen whether comprehensive results can be achieved with many of our ground-fossicking parrots and the much larger Australian cockatoo family.

No matter how good your management techniques are, sooner or later you will find that a problem will arise and whether it is a disease or structural (broken wings and legs, gashes etc.) you will require the services of an avian veterinarian. Good management therefore dictates whether you have just a pair of birds or hundreds, that you find out where your nearest bird vet is and place his or her telephone number where you will easily find it in an emergency.

1 - WILSON MOORE

1 - These aviaries have a grass floor. The walkway is at the rear.
2 - This large bank of aviaries is built on an angle so when the owner walks in one end and out the other he is still not too far from where he started.

2 - WILSON MOORE

1 - Non toxic timber poles provide a lovely rustic look to aviaries. Tin and an electric fence around the base control vermin.
2 - This typical small, neat aviary complex is well protected from the weather.
3 - A closer look into the bank of aviaries shown on opposite page. They are very clean and uncluttered. All drinking bowls are flushed at the turn of a tap.
4 - This type of complex is extremely popular in Australia. The flights can be serviced from front and rear walkways.

Managing Diseases and Injuries

The topic of diseases in aviary birds is not only gigantic but also extremely complex. It is beyond both my own knowledge of avian diseases and the realms of this book to cover this aspect in any worthwhile detail. However, having said that, a great deal of observation and common sense is required to be able to detect the sometimes very subtle changes in an unwell bird. I make it my own policy to concentrate on the well being and breeding of my birds, while if any do become either sick or injured, rather than trust my own limited knowledge, I take them to the vet immediately. Any aviculturist observing any problems with his stock is better to get them to an avian vet rather than fool around, perhaps giving antibiotics or pet shop remedies for ailments that even a qualified vet would have to do faecal tests, blood tests, X-Rays etc. to establish what the problem is. By all means we must learn by our experiences; records are invaluable when a similar thing crops up in the future and if ever a vet is not available then we can apply what knowledge we have gleaned by past experience. The application of that knowledge may just save a life. This is particularly so with injuries; broken wings or legs can sometimes be mended with success if one has been shown how to splint it and restrain the bird correctly in the past.

Many problems seem to occur just after purchasing birds and/ or releasing them into an area where other birds are kept. This may happen for several reasons. The first step in avoiding these problems is not to purchase sick or potentially sick birds: before even bringing the birds home they need a basic check over to determine that they at least look in good health. Before even removing the proposed purchase from its cage or aviary make certain that it is not fluffed up, unduly sleepy (with both feet on the perch, a healthy bird will sleep with its head tucked under a wing and stand on just one foot) or sluggish when all other birds around it are excited by your presence. Are they properly feathered, with no signs of feather plucking or diseased feathers (French moult, Psittacine beak and feather, cysts etc)? Broken feathers, unless excessive should not cause alarm if the bird is otherwise healthy. Chewed feathers though are a cause for concern. Broken feathers can be plucked out entirely and will be replaced by new ones in five to eight weeks. If they are left in, they will be replaced with new ones when the bird next moults. Look at both eyes very carefully to determine that they are clear and not watery. If you have seen it rubbing its eye along the perch in an effort to "scratch" an irritation, this is an indication of problems. Next, check that the bird has sufficient muscle on its chest, a healthy bird will be firm and meaty on either side of the sternum (chest bone). Its vent should show no signs of wetness or have faeces clinging to it or the surrounding feathers. Finally, legs, feet and toenails can be inspected for any damage or deformities. A golden rule is, if in doubt, do not take the bird. A reason for birds dying soon after coming into contact with new purchases is because the new arrivals have not been quarantined for at least three weeks in an area well away from your other stock. Doing this will produce signs of most illnesses if they are present before they can affect any other birds. If present, a visit to your vet and the appropriate treatment should see the bird back to good health. When it is well again, then and only then can the three week quarantining begin again. Some birds are carriers, that is they may carry a disease and while unaffected by it themselves, pass it on to other birds. Unfortunately, there is nothing, initially you can do to recognise a carrier until it is too late. When it has been established that a carrier does exist in your collection and has been positively identified, it should, without hesitation be taken to the vet and determined whether it can be cured, if not, it should put down, no matter how valuable the bird.

Finally, stress can play a major role in unwanted deaths. All species of birds carry unwanted germs, but because they are healthy their immune systems are able to cope with them. Stress can lower their immunity, just as a humans' is lowered when under stressful conditions. We may come down with a cold or flu but a bird will "come down" with ailments that can be a lot more serious than these. Birds, virtually thrown into an aviary with no thought as to its other occupants, its neighbours or its new environment as a whole, can have devastating consequences. Every care should be taken to make sure that the transition from the pet store or aviculturist is as smooth, quiet and untraumatising as possible.

So, good management includes:

1. Checking your prospective purchase over.

2. Quarantine all new arrivals.

3. Cleanliness and safely placed aviary fittings.

4. Close observation for different behaviour or demeanour.

5. Keep stressful situations to their absolute minimum.

6. Take ill birds to your avian vet. Telephoning the details through are not always good enough, you may not be able to recognise all the symptoms and of course a vet cannot do his or her job justice if unable to even conduct a blood or faecal analysis. You can aid your vet in diagnosing the problem by taking along with you a fresh sample of faeces, food & water.

A guide to worming dose rates

Species	Average Weight	Name & Volume of Anthelminthic		
		Levamisole	Panacur	Ivermectin
		1.4 (0.1mL/ 100gm)	2.5 (0.2mL/ 100gm)	(1:100) (0.2mL 100g)
Kings	200-230	0.2	0.4	0.4
Crimson-wings	150-170	0.15	0.3	0.3
Regents	160-180	0.15	0.3	0.3
Superbs	125-150	0.15	0.25	0.25
Princess	100-120	0.1	0.2	0.2
Mallee Ringnecks	120-140	0.1	0.2	0.2
Cloncurries	120-130	0.1	0.2	0.2
Twenty-eights	150-180	0.15	0.3	0.3
Port Lincolns	150-160	0.15	0.3	0.3
Red-caps	100-130	0.1	0.2	0.2
Kakarikis	60-90	0.05	0.1	0.1

All above dose rates are given orally with crop needle.

The weights of the above birds vary enormously in aviculture. It is therefore advisable for the reader to weigh his own birds to determine proper dose rate. One of the most convenient methods of weighing a bird is to: **1.** Weigh an empty cage. **2.** Put bird in cage and weigh. **3.** Substract weight 1 from weight 2.

N.B. There has been no scientific studies done on the useage of above mentioned anthelminthics on birds, and therefore the use of these drugs must remain the responsibility of the owner of birds.

Caring For New Arrivals

Bringing home new arrivals is always exciting! Shortly thereafter can be a time of heartbreak. Often in our excitement and enthusiasm we neglect to care for our new acquisitions in the best manner and subsequent sickness and deaths occur. Instinctively, we blame the supplier for not having sold us birds that were in the best of health, whereas in fact they may have been extremely healthy but because of the stress of being moved, change of diet, hotter/cooler climate, their natural immunity is lowered and they "pick up" something.

Many bacteria lie dormant in birds, not harming them or other birds at all but, will raise their ugly heads once the birds are put under varying amounts of stress. The obvious key then to make sure the healthy birds you bought remain healthy, is to settle them into their new environment as quickly and smoothly as possible.

Before bringing new arrivals home their cage or aviary should be thoroughly cleaned and disinfected, making sure that all washed perches are completely dry. Fresh water, seed and suitable fruits and vegetables (any diet that they may have already been on) should all be in place. Attention needs also to be given to the carrying cage that the birds are being transported in. It defeats the purpose to have an exceptionally clean aviary at home but the birds have been collected in a carry box that may never have been scrubbed out in its life. Many times I have seen people buying birds from breeders and dealers, carrying in their hands boxes that are full of old seed, wizened up fruit and dried faeces. Even after taking ill birds to a veterinarian, some people do not thoroughly clean out their carry boxes. This is asking for trouble! Quarantining new arrivals is always good policy. As stated earlier though, stress can itself bring about problems. Make certain that the quarantine cage is not so unsuitable that this in itself will bring on stress. Assuming the birds will only be housed this way for about three weeks and will therefore be alright is incorrect and certainly not good management. An unsuitable cage may be one that is too small and, if the birds are very flighty they will be extremely upset every time you change their food and water. It may be one that is in an area that is noisy, too hot, too cold or where a weaker bird can find no escape from its dominant mate. Different birds from different sources will take varying lengths of time to settle down in their new environment. Some will adapt extremely quickly, almost as though they were never moved. However some may take weeks or even months to adjust. Offering a diet that is the same or similar to that which they were being fed will make the transition easier. If you want to change the diet, it can be done at a later date when the birds are more accustomed to their new home. The sensible approach would also command that peace and quiet reign at least for the first few days. Children, dogs and especially cats should all be rigidly kept well away. Your new occupants will be well served if you set your feeding and cleaning habits to a pattern. If you adopt a routine from the outset and it is carried out slowly and sensibly with no sudden movements, it will help to reassure nervous birds.

All new acquisitions need to be observed very closely for the first week or two, this is when problems if they are going to occur probably will. Watch their eating habits, droppings and their general demeanour. Any change in these may indicate something is wrong. If any abnormal behaviour or suspicious droppings are observed, see your avian veterinarian immediately.

How old are your birds?

Until a bird attains its full adult plumage it is usually easily recognised as a juvenile. It may have an overall duller colouring than adults, different coloured beak, eyes and/or skin or may not have developed specific markings that only come with a certain age i.e., the yellow and red throat bands of the Superb Parrot *Polytelis swainsonii*.

Unless you know the exact history of a bird or it is close-rung with its year of birth imprinted on the band, it is practically impossible to know the bird's correct age. I have seen some older

1 - A 'D' feeder hung in the corner of the aviary reduces the possibility of birds fouling their drinking water.

2 - A wide variety of fruits and vegetables should be offered daily to our birds. Even if some of these are quite low in nutrition they are invaluable "Activity" foods.

3 - Parrots waste a great deal of food. Presenting it chopped into bite-sized pieces makes it easily handled by the birds with less falling to the ground.

birds well into their teens that are in excellent condition, and still breeding, that appear as though they could be markedly younger than others that I know are, but not in as good condition. Some more mature birds will show a little more scaling on the feet and legs while others may display some feather loss where the skin joins the beak. Even this feather loss around the beak may be misleading though, I once had a young Blue Princess Parrot that, in only its second year started losing a great deal of feathers from not only around its beak but also around its eyes. A visit to the vet revealed that it was a hormone imbalance and obviously not old age. So, ascertaining the age of most birds is purely guesswork, therefore, unless you know the background of prospective purchases, buy only birds that are obviously young.

Doing so will enable you to keep accurate records that will not only benefit you and perhaps the avicultural fraternity later, but may also make it easier to sell them when and if you so desire.

Diet and Nutrition

The exact nutritional requirements for each species of parrot is not yet known, however, as knowledge in this area rapidly grows we are realising that the more we learn of nutrition the more complicated and complex it appears to be, yet a "must' for them to thrive. We are though, abundantly aware that nutritional deficiencies are the most common cause of many diseases in parrots. Most of these diseases being a secondary problem that is directly traceable to improper nutrition. Therefore aviculturists should avail themselves of all the knowledge they can to keep their charges in the best of health, avoiding any problems. These problems do not occur overnight or in just a day or two, it is only after the normal body reserves of vitamins and minerals are depleted that the owner may start to notice something is awry. Malnourishment in birds even though they may appear in good condition can cause constipation, impaction and predispose bacterial or viral infections. More noticeable problems that can have their root cause in malnutrition are rickets, beak deformities, goitre and severe feather loss. A bird may suddenly die for no apparent reason. Only a trip to your avian veterinarian for an autopsy on the victim will reveal the exact cause. At this juncture it may well be wise to ask the vet if the particular cause of death could have been brought about by a nutritional deficiency, you may be surprised by the answer. Birds that are maintained in good health will not only radiate vigour and vitality but will also have the internal strength and fortitude to naturally resist all but the most diabolical diseases.

As mentioned, the subject is a complex one and would most certainly fill more than even a few books. The subject nevertheless is of such significance to the modern aviculturist that no book covering the care and breeding of parrots should neglect it, albeit at a very basic level. The application of these nutritional needs even at this level will aid any aviculturist in raising, maintaining and breeding his birds.

Quite apart from these nutritional requirements, birds, like people, probably get tired of eating the same old food offered day in and day out, especially if it consists of little more than dry seed.

If you offer a variety of good food and display a measure of patience you will gradually discover what your birds will eat. Birds can eat most of the things we do and most of them are good for them. Learn what they are, but be mindful not to spoil them with foods that are low nutritionally in place of those that it needs to maintain good health.

Nutritional Requirements of Young Birds

1. Newborn chicks require 25-28% of their body weight each day of food (dry weight) for the first 3 days. This needs to be given in a 93% water solution (7% solids) fed each 3 hours between 6.30am and 11pm and once through the night at about 3am.

2. After three days you can then feed approximately 30% solids right up till weaning. This percentage of food to water may vary slightly though depending on the formula that you are using, some naturally absorbing more liquid than others. Variations though should not be extreme.

1 - KEVIN WILSON

3. Protein requirements for maximum growth is 20% in a starch (cereal) base. If the percentage gets any lower than 15%, stunting occurs. At 10% birds may start to die and at a level as low as 5% all young birds will die at about two to three weeks of age. On the other end of the scale, too much protein can also be detrimental: at 25-35% behavioural changes will eventuate such as biting, nervousness, rejection of feeding and regurgitation at peak weight and age (three to five weeks). Chicks at a younger age fed 35% protein reflect a depressed growth rate. On 20-25% protein chicks grow well.

4. Fat is the substance stored by the body, assimilated by the intake of food over and above the body's requirements for energy, growth and the rebuilding of cells. Young parrots have fat requirements in small quantities. 3.75% is all that is necessary as a reserve source of body heat and energy and as a cushion for the body, particularly for vital organs, muscles and nerves. It is only when a diet contains higher than 60% fats will it become detrimental.

5. Any diet fed to birds young or mature must contain a complete vitamin and mineral mix. Their importance cannot be stressed enough. Choline and riboflavin deficiency cause achromatosis (no pigment in the feathers). Lysine and pantothenic acid are essential for normal growth, body weight gain and survival. Vitamin K is particularly important when feeding chicks for the first three days. This can be added in the form of yoghurt or boiled spinach. It must be boiled first to remove the effects of oxalic acid which inhibits the absorption of calcium. An alternative to cooking fresh spinach is to use a commercial baby food. Calcium requirements should be balanced at 2-1 ratio with phosphorus. Calcium should be given at 1-2% dry weight and phosphorus at 0.7-1.2% of the diet. Phosphorus forms part of every cell in the body and is therefore an essential bulk element in nutrition. A bird's egg contains over 25% phosphorus, making it the most abundant mineral contained within it. Just about all foods that are high in protein are also high in phosphorus. Bird's

1 - Cloncurry chicks at just 12 days old.

diets that are supplemented with small amounts of peanuts, egg, walnuts and sunflower seed are rich in phosphorus. Most fruits and vegetables on the other hand, are low in phosphorus.

Although phosphorus is vitally important to life, deficiencies rarely if ever occur under normal conditions. Only a gross imbalance in the calcium to phosphorus ratio or a vitamin D deficiency in the diet may cause any problem. This could result in rickets, growth failure, loss of appetite, weakness and death in extremely severe cases.

Pelleted Diets

I am addressing pelleted diets briefly because at the time of writing such a product is about to be marketed in Australia. The trend overseas, particularly in the United States is to package nutrition in neatly formed pellets. Chickens and other animals have been fed successfully on pelleted diets for many years now and manufacturers claim, in most instances that they are "complete" diets. The balanced diet contained therein is all that is required to maintain birds at their peak of health. The drift towards this idea will undoubtedly reach these shores sooner or later. Food presented in this manner certainly has some advantages. Medication becomes so much easier. The finicky dietary needs of specific species becomes easier to fulfill e.g. insectivorous birds, flamingoes, kingfishers, waders etc as well as making preparation time much less tedious for those with larger collections. Therefore pelleted diets are ideal as far as zoos and large collections are concerned.

My personal objection to feeding these artificial diets is that they perhaps rob the birds of some aspects in their life that are probably equally as important as a balanced diet. Firstly, I believe that the emotional well being of a parrot is extremely important. As is with humans, if we are mentally well and happy, then likely we are also physically well. Parrots in captivity have a great deal of time on their hands, often with not much to do. Providing them with anything that stimulates mental and physical activity can only be beneficial to them and a variety of food shapes, sizes, textures and tastes will contribute to this.

Secondly, it may tend to make the aviculturist a little lazy as well as depriving him or her of very rewarding experiences and observations while doling out "fresh" food. A sick bird, unusual mating behaviour or nesting activity may well be missed by those not taking the time to feed at least once or twice daily. Some parrots adore these pellets while others reluctantly eat them. It has also been recorded that some birds, no matter how close to death by starvation they become, will still not take them.

Parrots comprise one of the largest groups of so called "seed eating" birds in captivity. Any animal or bird that eats seed only is termed "granivorous", parrots however are most definitely omnivorous, that is they eat a variety of foods. The bird keeper who is trying to formulate a balanced diet for his parrots will need to provide a wide range of foodstuffs. This is usually done by giving ad lib a particular assortment. This means the bird is left to sort out its own requirements. Just as with labour saving seed hoppers and the like, the birds are left to pick out just the seeds they enjoy the most. However a better way would be to feed the birds twice daily, only what they can eat and no more. This controlled way of feeding, although taking more time, allows you to feed them a balanced diet.

All of the birds discussed in this book can and should be offered all the foods listed below in varying amounts as suggested.

Ideally, where applicable they should be cut into 1 to 2cm cubes for easier handling by the birds and can be mixed together and presented fresh at least once a day, preferably twice. These foods should be given more frequently and in larger quantities when the birds are breeding, moulting, recuperating or going through any form of stress. Otherwise it can be considered a maintenance diet.

As an additional supplement I also give those birds that will eat it a piece of specially baked nutritional cake. Non-breeding birds will get a piece once per week while those with young eagerly take a piece every day.

The recipe is as follows:-

2 Cups of oats
2 Cups of dried milk powder
2 Cups of wholemeal flour
1 Cup of soya flour
1 Cup of crushed mixed nuts
1/2 Cup of rice cereal
4 Tablespoons of peanut butter
4 Tablespoons of wheatgerm
6 Tablespoons of honey
4 Teaspoons of calcium carbonate
6 Eggs

Method (All ingredients)

Add enough water to make a mix the consistency of a regular cake mix. Place into cake pans to a depth of about 50mm (2in). Place in the oven at 190 degrees F for about 45 minutes or until cooked. When cool, slice into small cubes and store in freezer.

Thaw out as required and present to the birds in a little milk.

One pair of birds feeding young may consume between the equivalent of one or two 2.5cm (1in) squares of cake per day.

Dietary Components

Dry seeds	
Feed Daily	
Canary	Hulled Oats
Sunflower	White Millet
Jap Millet	Yellow Millet
Safflower	Niger & Rape
Corn	Oats

Nuts	
Feed once or twice every month	
Peanuts	Almonds

Supplementary Protein	
Feed once every two weeks	
Dog food (Dried & canned)	
Cooked Chicken & bones	

Tinned Tuna fish
High protein Baby foods
Cheese   Cooked Chop bones

Vegetables

Feed Daily

Capsicum	Peppers
Silver beet	Endive
Lettuce	Cabbage
Celery	Carrot
Lucerne- Alfalfa	Peas
Seeding grasses	Wild Berries

Silver Beet should be cooked first (boiled for a couple of minutes) to eliminate oxalic acid which prevents the utilisation of calcium. Carrots also need to be boiled to release their vitamin and mineral content. Cabbage, it is thought may have an anti-thyroid effect.

Fruit

Feed Daily

Apple	Orange
Pear	Banana
Strawberries	Paw-paw
Stoned fruits (not avocados)	

Fruits are fed to parrots more for variety than any great nutritional value, particularly so with those high in water content. Avocados have been responsible for the death of some varieties of birds and should be avoided.

Live food

Feed weekly to those that will eat them

Mealworms	Lerps
Caterpillars	
Other insects and their larvae	

Live food is not taken by all parrots but seems to be an individual preference, it is nevertheless high in protein.

Soaked and Sprouted Seeds

Feed Daily

Soak seed for twenty four hours in water to soften it and make it more palatable for all parrots, especially those with young and those that are weaning. After soaking it must be rinsed thoroughly and all excess water shaken off. Present only the amount that will be consumed in a relatively short period of time because if left it may go "off".

For the seed to go into its second phase, sprouting, it needs to be kept warm and rinsed frequently. If it is not kept clean while going through this stage, mould growth, fermentation and the production of aflatoxins will occur.

Sprouted seeds change nutritionally, their protein value is immensely increased making it a valuable food during breeding when a bird's protein reserves are most likely to be quite low. But don't forget, soaked and sprouted seeds are extremely perishable, at the first hint of an "off" smell or mould they must be discarded.

Pulses

Feed Daily

Peas   Mung & other beans
Lentils

A variety of assorted peas, lentils and beans can be soaked or sprouted and offered to your parrots. This can be done in the same manner as soaked and sprouted seed.

Cuttle Bone

Offered Ad Lib

Good quality, clean and dry cuttle bone contains many of the required minerals for maintenance, growth and egg production. Nearly all egg laying hens will consume quantities of fresh cuttle bone but those that lack enthusiasm for it are likely to eventually have shell abnormalities. Studies have proven a direct relationship.

Grit

Offered Ad Lib

All parrots have crops in which the food, particularly seeds, is masticated before it proceeds along the intestinal tract. To aid this maceration, a fine grit (up to 2mm in diameter) is necessary. Washed river sand is ideal.

Water

Offered Ad Lib

Fresh water is most important for parrots in captivity. In the wild if water is unavailable for any length of time they can still extract a certain amount of moisture from plants and foliage. In an aviary these may not always be readily available. Clean water, free from droppings that will cause infections, should be replenished every day. Water soluble vitamin and mineral preparations are ill advised, as **1.** when exposed to sunlight have a very short life, therefore, are a waste of money. **2.** Create a dangerous growth medium for unwanted bacteria. **3.** often have a bitter taste making the taking of fluids undesirable for the birds. Powdered vitamin and mineral preparations are best fed mixed or sprinkled on soft foods that are consumed the same day.

Sunlight

Sunlight is a requirement of all parrots to convert provitamin D into vitamin D3, necessary for the absorption of calcium, since vitamin D occurs too irregularly in our captive birds' diet. When exposed to the ultra violet rays of the sun this provitamin (7-dehydrocholesterol) is synthesised and travels to the skin surface where it is converted to cholecalciferol or vitamin D3.

Vitamins and Minerals at a glance

Vitamin A

Is essential for maintaining tissue growth and good eyesight. It keeps the skin and bones healthy. Lack of it often causes mouth and throat lesions (e.g. Candida albicans) and defects in eye functions.

Source: Eggs, vegetables, fruit and milk.

B1 Thiamine

Aids important metabolic functions, overall growth, muscle texture and a healthy nervous system. Lack of it commonly causes leg paralysis, poor appetite, digestive problems and general weakness.

Source: Cereal grains, green vegetables, wheat, peas and beans.

B2 Riboflavin

Aids important metabolic functions, skin, feather and nail quality. Deficiency causes curled toes and paralysis.

Source: Milk, egg white, wheat germ, cheese, green vegetables.

B3 Niacin

Needed for the metabolic processes, the nervous and digestive systems as well as for the production of hormones. Inadequacies lead to slow growth, poor feather quality and scaly dermatitis.

Source: Grains and nuts.

B6 Pyridoxine

Helps with the production of digestive juices, the development of red blood cells and antibodies as well as the operation of nervous and musculoskeletal systems. Insufficiency causes a lack of appetite and weight as well as impaired reproduction.

Source: Green vegetables, whole grains.

B12 Cyanoco-balamin

Necessary for normal metabolism. Its absence leads to impaired egg hatchability, bone deformities and growth retardation.

Source: Egg yolk.

Biotin

Assists in important metabolic functions. Shortage can impair egg hatchability, cause bone deformities and skin diseases.

Source: Nuts and whole grains.

Choline

Aids in metabolising fats and cholesterol as well as helping with the functioning of the nervous system, liver and kidneys. Its depletion leads to kidney and liver ailments, fatty liver degeneration, slipped tendon and hock disease.

Source: Green vegetables, egg yolk.

Folic Acid

Aids the body in its use of proteins and helps with the production of red blood cells and body tissue. Its need can cause anaemia, loss of pigmentation and retarded body and feather growth.

Source: Whole grains, green vegetables.

Pantothenic Acid

A must for cellular metabolism, a healthy digestive tract and proper functioning of the adrenal glands. Lack of it results in retarded growth and feather development, skin ailment and diseases as well as liver damage and impaired egg hatchability.

Source: Peanuts, green vegetables, whole grains.

Vitamin C

Helps with connective tissue formation, healing injuries and fighting infection and assists with the production of red blood cells. Its depletion has no ill effect on most psittacines except that it may cause scurvy in fruit and nectar eaters.

Source: Citrus fruits, tomatoes, raw green vegetables.

Vitamin D3

Because birds cannot utilise vitamin D2 they must have D3 for proper bone formation, a sound heart and nervous system and to aid blood clotting. It is essential to prevent rickets, soft shelled eggs and egg binding because it enables calcium absorption.

Source: Direct sunlight (see page 21) whole milk, fish oils, egg yolk.

Vitamin E

Increases fertility, blood circulation and the regeneration of tissue. It is also an antioxidant and prevents the degeneration of fatty acids and vitamins A and D. Deficiency leads to decreased fertility, degenerative muscle disease and softening of the brain. Its depletion also causes acute itchiness, glandular enlargement and edema.

Source: Wheat germ, green vegetables, eggs, soya beans, peanuts.

Vitamin K

Essential for the proper functioning of liver, for blood clotting and general vitality of the bird. Deficiency can lead to poor blood clotting.

Source: Green vegetables, egg yolk, soya beans.

Minerals

Calcium

Essential for the development and growth of both bones and muscles. Aids the proper functioning of the heart, muscles, blood and nervous system. Lack of calcium produces poor bone growth and bones that deform, bend or fracture easily.

Source: Milk, cheese, cuttlefish bone.

Chlorine

Needed to maintain the correct alkali acid and fluid balance as well as producing stomach acids. Deficiency causes upset in the balance of alkali acid, improper digestion and loss of body fluids.

Source: Common salt, shell grit.

Iodine

Regulates metabolism, a must for thyroidal production of the thyroxine hormone. Omission of Iodine causes enlarged thyroid and parathyroid glands, also hindering other metabolic functions.

Source: Seafood and kelp.

Iron

Iron is part of the haemoglobin in red blood cells that carries the oxygen, therefore is essential to the development and function of healthy blood. Low Iron content causes anaemia and debilitated transportation of oxygen from the lungs to the tissue, muscle weakness and poor operation of the whole body.

Source: Cooked red meat, nuts, green vegetables, soya beans.

Magnesium

Valuable for bone formation and proper metabolism, also activates enzymes. Depletion impairs bone formation, the usage of carbohydrates and amino acids.

Source: Whole grains, vegetables, fruits, nuts, beans.

Manganese

Also valuable for bone and blood formation and regulating metabolism by activating enzymes. Insufficient quantities lead to bone disease, anaemia, poor body metabolism and general weakness.

Source: Green vegetables, whole grains, nuts.

Phosphorus

Fundamental for important metabolic functions, the growth of cells and their regeneration, the digestion of vitamins B2 and B3 and combines with calcium in the formation of bones. Lack of phosphorous causes poor bone formation and bone disease, also poor tissue healing and body sores.

Source: Whole grains, nuts, eggs, seeds, vegetables.

Selenium

A co-worker with vitamin E and it is possible that it may have some anti-cancer properties. Insufficient amounts can lead to poor tissue healing and muscle deterioration.

Source: Wheat germ.

Sodium

Helps to regulate the bodies' fluids and keep an alkali acid balance. Subnormal amounts causes dehydration and an upset in the alkali acid ratio.

Source: Root vegetables, eggs and as common salt.

Zinc

Zinc is necessary for normal metabolism and is a component of insulin. Its deficiency upsets body metabolism and causes diabetes mellitus through a decrease in insulin production.

Source: Vegetables, wheat germ, nuts.

Failure To Breed

All healthy birds have an in built instinct to breed. If they fail to do so you must explore every aspect of your setup to discover why they are not. All birds breed with varying amounts of difficulty or ease. Aviculturists need to do all they can to assist in providing all that is necessary for them to produce eggs, incubate, hatch and raise strong, healthy chicks. The following chart may help you to overcome possible reasons for not breeding.

Possible Reason	Possible Remedy
Not a true pair (cock and hen).	*If sexual dimorphism (different colouration in male and female) is not apparent, the only way to be certain that you have a pair is to have them surgically sexed by an avian veterinary surgeon. It is a simple and relatively inexpensive job with little or no risk involved.*
Too young or too old	*Different birds mature sexually at different ages. Some will breed while still in their immature colours, while others will not breed until in their third or fourth year. Most of the birds discussed in this book will be old enough to breed successfully in their second year. If a bird is too old, nothing of course will remedy this. Remember though, that some of the birds discussed have an amazingly long breeding life, twenty years and more.*
Incompatibility	*Sometimes a female, no matter what is done just will not accept a particular male. If this is the case it is usually evident in all other behaviour. They may not sit together, preen each other or feed together. They may avoid each others company at all times and at all costs, squabbling if their paths do cross too closely. A change of partner is suggested. Sometimes, either bird may be very particular in which case further changes may bring about the desired results. Remember not to be too hasty in changing partners though, as some birds take a year or more to "settle in" before they attempt to breed.*
Hen not satisfied with nesting arrangements	*King Parrots are one of the most difficult to please when it comes to both nest site and choice of box or log, less so with other species. Before the breeding season commences, place a choice of logs and boxes of differing sizes in a variety of positions throughout the aviary. When and if one is chosen, all others should be removed. A nesting box or log may be favoured and selected by a hen but will still show reluctance to go down, if so, she may be dissatisfied with the position it is hanging in. If so try it somewhere else.*
Out of breeding condition	*To mate, lay eggs and produce healthy, young offspring, birds need to be in prime condition during that particular species' breeding season. If they are moulting or have not been fed a suitable diet that will bring both birds simultaneously into peak condition at the appropriate time, they will not usually go to nest. If they have been sick or for some other reason have been under stress, this too will put them out of condition. Many species in the wild attain their peak condition from the types and availability of certain foods prior to and during the breeding season. By providing a diet that furnishes all the appropriate proteins, carbohydrates, fats, vitamins and minerals, you can build up your bird's condition to its peak just at the right time.*
Lack of stimulus	*Most serious aviculturists specialise and therefore have more than one pair of a particular species. One main reason for this is that*

some birds are encouraged to breed by the sound and behaviour of other birds of their own kind nearby. Some birds that have not bred for years or at all as an only pair have reacted favourably as soon as they were stimulated by others. Certain foods too may stimulate them. Study what foods are available to them in the wild at that particular time of the year and as far as you can, provide it. For example I have found that Princess Parrots and Kakarikis like most birds need more protein prior to breeding, and offering live meal worms provides this as well as stimulating them to breed. In recent years it has become, to some extent, fashionable to use metal or plastic nesting boxes. If you are using one of these, try changing to a natural log or a wooden box as, in most parrots, wood chewing is also a pre-breeding stimulus.

A compatible pair is one of the first steps to successful breeding.

WILSON MOORE

Insufficient privacy.

Many aviaries designed and built in Australia for parrots give little thought to privacy. A well designed one will, and that may be all that is necessary to encourage some shy birds to mate and commence nesting. An area that birds can "hide" in is easy to supply. A simple partition or even a log placed appropriately to give seclusion will suffice. Protection against annoying or noisy cats, dogs or children is also a positive step in giving them adequate privacy in which to breed.

Mixed aviaries.

Mixed collections rarely work well if you want your birds to breed. Nest stealing, hogging vital food supplies, on the wrong end of the pecking order and other disturbances all add to the failure of breeding. Ideally, house one pair of birds per aviary or, if a species that will colony breed, house just that particular species together.

Inappropriate neighbours.

Even if double wire is used to protect one pair of birds against the aggressive behaviour of their neighbours, upsets in breeding can still occur if they are of the same or even related species. You may find the male in one flight is more interested in the female next door than in his own mate. If possible, arrange your birds so that totally unrelated species are housed adjacent to each other and do this well before the season commences.

Sick birds.

Sick birds cannot be expected to breed. If throughout winter you have experienced ongoing problems, attend to them immediately. An avian veterinarian will test your bird's blood and faeces and instigate cultures that can determine the health of your bird very quickly. He can administer healing procedures that may soon overcome their inability to breed. Calcium deficiency, hormone imbalance, infections, prolapses, hernias and tumours are just a few of the ailments that can prevent satisfactory breeding.

Hand Rearing

There are many reasons that an aviculturist is called upon to hand rear a single or whole brood of chicks. It can be a decision that has been thoroughly thought out and prepared for, or a situation that has been forced upon you leaving you with little or no choice at all. A chick that has been ousted from its nest or a brood that "mother" has decided she will no longer feed usually spawns panic in the heart of the novice breeder. Whatever the reason is that you may be called upon to take up such a task, you must remember that it is very time consuming, especially with chicks that are only a day or so old, and therefore severely restricts for a time, most other activities. The rewards, on the other hand can be tremendous. Not only does one have a delightfully tame bird that often enjoys your company as much as you enjoy its, but you are blessed, contrary to many peoples way of thinking, with a bird that by far makes a better and steadier breeder. Rarely is a tame, sitting female ever put off her eggs or young by disturbances. Some breeders are now doing their utmost to obtain only hand raised birds as they have found their qualities are far better than flightier, parent raised birds.

The need for heat and humidity

A new born chick requires a temperature of between 33 and 37 degrees C. As the chick grows and produces feathers its need for heat diminishes. Chicks with heavy down will need less warmth than those that are born naked. In some climates an incubator or brooder is needed to maintain the appropriate temperature, in others, only a heat pad is sufficient, like those sold in the pet trade for elderly or debilitated cats and dogs. If a commercially built brooder is not available to you then a simple, practical brooder can easily be made from a glass or plastic fish

1 - WILSON MOORE

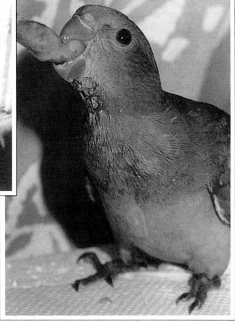

2 - KEVIN WILSON

1 - Princess chicks a few days old will require to be kept artificially warm if removed for hand-rearing.
2 - Spoon fed youngsters like this Regent Parrot make terrific pets that adore their owners.

tank or a laminated wooden box. Untreated wood or cardboard is ill advised as it harbours germs and prevents adequate cleaning. The heat source can be, as mentioned, a heat pad or even a 15 watt light globe housed inside a tin can that is about 12cm (4.5in) across.

The sides of the can must only produce "warmth" and not enough heat to burn the chick if it snuggles up to it, which it will invariably do. Whatever method is used to warm the brooder the heat can be kept in by a simple lid on top made from a sheet of polystyrene with air holes punched in or even a towel drooped across the top with a small gap for air. Whether a heat pad or light globe is used as a heat source, much greater control is achieved by fixing a dimmer control switch to the wiring. It is a simple and relatively inexpensive item that will make your task of controlling the heat a whole lot easier.

Maintaining the correct temperature requirements of chicks is important and depends a great deal upon many factors such as age, species, the climate from which the chick came and the number of chicks being raised. A single chick will require more heat than two or more, as these will generate some considerable warmth of their own. Watch your charges carefully. A chick that is too hot will start to turn red and its skin will turn wrinkly. With chicks that are covered in thick down, these signs may not be readily seen, so I repeat, watch them carefully. If left too warm for any long periods they start to exhibit restless behaviour, continually hurling themselves about as though in a stupor often panting or gasping. In an effort to escape the heat, a group of chicks, instead of being huddled together will disperse to the outer perimeters of their brooder. When a heat pad is used I only have it under two thirds of the brooder, leaving an area that is a little cooler which the chicks will manage to find if necessary.

If it is too cold, the chick will feel cool or cold to the touch and appears extremely lethargic. When fed, it will take more than the proper time for the food to empty from the crop. This may lead to sour crop, an impaction of food that will not digest and is extremely difficult to move and, if not, may result in death.

Too low temperatures will also retard growth and the chicks resistance to disease will be lowered. When a young bird is being raised at the right temperature it will spend most of its time, at least until it is almost fully feathered, sleeping or resting contentedly. A quality thermometer or two is needed or better still and even more accurate a thermometer with a digital readout. Don't rely on your own senses; a chick that is too hot or too cold will die.

The floor of the brooder should be lined with fine wood shavings and on top of this a layer of paper towelling that is of the un-bleached variety. Bleached towels tend to "burn" tender young skin. The purpose of paper towelling is to monitor the bowel movements of the young bird, its regularity and consistency. Chicks also have a need for about 80% humidity in their atmosphere. They rehydrate themselves by breathing in humid air.

A brooder soon becomes depleted of moisture if it is not replaced. This can be done quite simply by placing a small jar or bowl of water in the brooder with the birds. If a jar with a screw cap is used, holes can be punched or drilled into the cap.

Cover a bowl with wire to prevent youngsters from falling in, make certain though, that there are no sharp edges to the wire that can tear the delicate skin of these tender aged chicks. This arrangement will give the approximate amount of humidity required. If you want to be more accurate then you can purchase a wet bulb thermometer designed to measure humidity.

Feeding Formulas

There seem to be as many different formulas for hand raising birds as there are birds. But this will not help the newcomer to hand-rearing, he or she has to start somewhere. Over the past few years I have been using as a base mix, a commercially made product called Wombaroo*™ "granivore". It is a powdered product that needs only warm water added to it to be used. It is made specifically for rearing grain eating birds and I simply add to it various slurries of blended fruits and vegetables depending on the species. For example, a species that naturally consume larger quantities of fruits and vegetable matter, like the Eclectus Parrot, I would add about 30% blended apple, pear, orange, capsicum, carrot and stoned fruits as well as a few drops of calcium each day. Cockatiels though, being mainly seed eaters can be reared fully on the Wombaroo*™ diet alone. It contains all the basic requirements including protein, fat, carbohydrate, energy, vitamin A, vitamin D, vitamin E, ascorbate, thiamine, riboflavin, nicotinamide, pantothenate, pyridoxine, vitamin B12, folate, biotin, calcium, phosphorus, sodium, potassium, magnesium, iron, manganese and copper. One of the many formulas I have also used with complete success is made by blending together the following ingredients:

> 1 pkt. Hi-protein baby cereal
> 1/2 pkt milk arrowroot biscuits
> 100 gms wheat germ
> 100 gms hulled sunflower kernels
> 200gms ground oats.

These ingredients are all blended to a fine powder and stored in an airtight container. When required, hot water is added and is then allowed to stand for a couple of minutes to "cook". If it is fed too quickly after mixing it will become too thick in the crop, consequently a little more water is added along with about 15% baby food of the meat and vegetable variety and another 15% of a fruit variety. It is important for this fruit to be added whether they are birds that would normally eat fruit in their natural habitat or not as a certain amount of fruit added will aid the digestion. Rarely do young birds fed a substantial amount of fruit in the diet suffer from a compacted crop. Once a day, one or two drops of Pentavite*™ childrens' vitamins (available from chemists) or an even better product in my opinion is Duphasol Plus*™ a liquid vitamin preparation made specifically for animals and is available from veterinarians, and liquid calcium (Calcium Sandoz syrup*™) available from pet or veterinary suppliers, are also added.

How much how often?

The consistency of the food will depend greatly upon the age of the bird. A youngster that is only a day or two old will only be able to handle an extremely thin, watery food every two hours if the crop has completely emptied. (See section on Nutritional requirements of young birds). New born chicks have only very small crops and will not hold much food at all. Don't force the chick to take more than it can handle. Remember they are very weak at this tender age and will eat very slowly and tire very quickly. At this very early age parrot chicks won't "pump" the food down but will rather tend to suck at the food. As the chick grows so the food should become thicker until it is about the consistency of sloppy porridge. Feeding intervals will be determined by the speed of the crop emptying. A King Parrot chick of about four to five weeks of age will need feeding about four times per day, starting at about 6 or 6.30am with the last feed about 11pm. The amount fed to any bird varies greatly, depending on the age, crop capacity and the individual enthusiasm to feed etc. A chick that feeds with great fervour will often not know when to stop and will continue to cry for feed even though the crop is bulging to capacity. It is unwise to fill any chick to this extent. Over feeding is dangerous and if you are unsure of how much to give, it is better to underfeed and give the next feed sooner, than to over feed and be tempted to feed again before the crop has fully emptied. Many would be hand raisers are daunted by the thought that it is necessary to get out of bed every night at two hourly intervals to feed several gaping mouths. This is not necessary, although some parrots and cockatoos do feed their young at night, they are probably only fed very small quantities. I have found in my own experience that only very young birds will need feeding at night, and then only once at about 2.30 or 3am.

1 - KEVIN WILSON

2 - KEVIN WILSON

1 - A home made brooder can be as simple as an aquarium with a suitable heating implement. The jar of water provides humidity.
2 - Amboinan/ Australian King Parrot chick being hand raised. Note the thick grey down that covers the body before pin feathers emerge.

Keeping the food warm

A bird's natural body temperature is around 40-42 degrees C., that is higher than our own. Most chicks tend to prefer their food a little warmer than we might assume (approximately 43 degrees C). If presented too cool, it will be unacceptable and refused. Too hot and severe damage may occur to the chicks crop by burning.

The above mentioned diets are heated when hot water is added. When the correct consistency is achieved by adding more or less water, the temperature can be maintained by placing the feeding cup or bowl within a larger bowl filled with warm water. The nature of these ground and powdered food preparations make it easy to prepare fresh food for each feeding. The fruit and vegetable part can be mixed and frozen in ice cube trays, popping out one cube at each feed to thaw out ready for the next feeding. Some breeders mix up quantities of the whole food and freeze it, then as required warm up in a saucepan or microwave oven the prepared food. If microwaves are used, care should be taken to stir in well any hot spots that may occur.

Utensils for feeding

For all the parrots dealt with in this book I have found that, even for chicks only hours old, the most practical utensil is a teaspoon. With its sides bent upwards, it forms a concave not unlike the lower mandible of an adult parrot. Some breeders prefer to use either a syringe or eye dropper on very young chicks and then move onto, when it is a week or two old, the spoon. Whichever method you use is not as important as the bird being able to consume its food quickly, while it remains warm and with the least amount of stress to either the bird or its feeder.

Sooner or later for the aviculturist who decides to hand rear a lot of birds each season, problems with feeding occur. When, for whatever reason, a chick decides it no longer wishes to eat, immediate action is warranted. A quick trip to your avian veterinarian should find the problem. A King Parrot I was hand

1 - KEVIN WILSON

1 - Syringe or bent spoon can be used to feed chicks. A more natural response is had when the bill like bent spoon is used.
2 - Crop needles are invaluable when de-worming or otherwise medicating parrots. They can also be used effectively to force feed chicks or adult parrots that are unable, through sickness, to feed themselves.

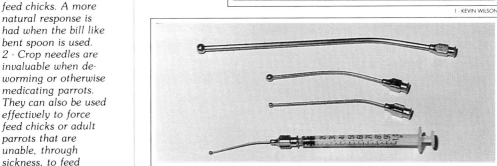

2 - KEVIN WILSON

rearing last year suddenly lost all desire to eat, the cause was diagnosed as "candida" by my vet and he provided me with the appropriate medicine. The original problem though still remained, he didn't want to eat his food. To overcome this, until he regained the urge to eat again, I decided to use a crop needle attached to a syringe. The size of this needle depends on the size and age of the chick.

Normally these instruments are used to carry medicines, especially de-worming agents directly to the crop. In this instance it was to carry life sustaining food. A slightly more liquid formula is made up and drawn up the crop needle into the body of the syringe. The needle has a round ball on the end with the outlet hole passing through it. This ball is there to protect the oesophagus and the crop from being pierced. The tip of the needle is very carefully placed over the birds tongue and down the oesophagus which runs down the birds right side into the crop. The plunger is then depressed to empty the contents into the crop. The novice hand raiser is not advised to attempt this method of feeding unless absolutely necessary, as, for the first time round it can be quite nerve rattling and will not only put undue stress upon you but the bird also. Before any hand raising is contemplated in this manner, have an experienced breeder or bird dealer show you exactly how it is done. Once you have accomplished it, it will come in extremely handy in administering other items, particularly de-worming agents as this is really the most effective way of doing this necessary task.

While I am discussing the crop needle it may be prudent to relate a further use. If sour crop (a firm lump of undigested food in the crop) is found after a few hours, it will need to be removed.

A small amount of molasses mixed with warm water (ratio 1-3) should be injected via the crop needle to the crop. A very gentle massaging of this liquid in the crop should break up the gluggy lump enough for it to be, extremely carefully drawn back up into the syringe. Again this procedure needs experience and great care. Any small amount of liquid molasses left in the crop should then go through the bird's system. Do not feed again for at least a couple of hours and even then only if its droppings are again coming through and then only with a very watery slurry to begin with. Continue feeding with a wetter mix and/or add a little more fruit to the diet, this should prevent the problem recurring.

Weaning

All of the parrots covered in this book normally wean at about eight to ten weeks of age, but this can be no real indication of some individuals. Some parrot chicks I have reared weaned remarkably quickly, in as little as 65 days while others seem to take forever, well into the twelfth week.

The first indications that they are ready to be weaned is the growing lack of interest in their food. They may take a couple of mouthfuls and then simply play with the spoon or reject it altogether, keeping beak firmly closed. When this behaviour begins, or even before, a variety of appropriate foods can be placed in a shallow dish on the floor of the brooder, or now that the chick is just about fully feathered, on the floor of a cage. Soft foods are ideal, corn kernels, peas, spinach, soft pear, carrot and sprouted mung beans should all be offered in small diced pieces.

Parrot mix containing sunflower, canary, oats and an assortment of millets can be soaked in water for twenty four hours, rinsed well and offered. The soaking makes the husks easy to break and weaning parrots will soon learn to extract the flesh, play with it for a while and then experiment with chewing it. These same foods (not the seed) can also be presented to them cooked. You can also blend them and offer a firm, crunchy mix in a dish on the floor, this may take their fancy quicker than "lumps" of food. Most important of all though is patience, don't be in too much of a hurry, the bird in its own time will experiment with it's food and eventually no longer take from the spoon at all.

During this time of weaning I suggest that you keep up at least three feeds from the spoon each day and rather than cut out a feed altogether, just lessen the quantity. This will encourage the bird to feed itself. When it is eating properly, swallowing food and not just playing with it, the feed given in the middle of the day can be eliminated, then the morning feed and eventually the evening meal. Some parrots will continue to enjoy a feed from the spoon every now and then. An Eclectus hen I have, although three years old and with her first batch of young in the nest, will still delight in being offered some tasty "slop" from the spoon. After fledging it never ceases to amaze me that when these chicks hatched they were so tiny, naked, blind and helpless. Yet miraculously within about four to six weeks they have grown astoundingly into immature versions of their parents that will soon be independent. Just because though, you have seen your chicks raised thus far without any problems does not mean that the next few weeks will not present any.

When young birds fledge into a very large aviary or the parent birds have bred in an aviary where they have had little or practically no human contact, the offspring can be extremely flighty. If they do not master their flying technique very quickly there is a possibility they may break their necks by flying headlong into the wire or perches. This disastrous problem can be overcome by hanging sacks or putting gum branches around the walls of the aviary to "cushion" the blows. The birds will be able to see them clearly and help avoid these air born disasters. With birds that are naturally steady like Princess or Regents or birds that are used to their keeper's comings and goings, this sort of problem doesn't usually arise.

After weaning it is time to give consideration to moving them to alternative accommodation. The reason for this is that some birds double brood (go to nest twice in the same season). If the parents wish to do so, they may well feel the youngsters are intruding and may become spiteful towards them. This is especially true of the male parent. When they have been moved they should be offered identical food as they and their parents were consuming in their original home.

Place them into their own accommodation early in the day so that they may become accustomed to it well before nightfall. For the first few days especially, watch them very carefully. Any sign of distress, illness or inability to feed themselves should be dealt with promptly. Never leave any bird that appears unwell to see if it "comes good" on its own, they rarely do. In many cases it may only be a slight chill with a short spell in a heated hospital cage aiding its full recovery.

Security

Security is not so much from the aspect of birds escaping, although this is obviously important but more from the angle of keeping people out.

Keeping your birds safe from either thieves or well meaning but misinformed animal liberationists, can be a daunting task. Most smaller collections are usually safe, apart from perhaps the odd vandal. It is usually the more valuable birds and larger collections that are targeted. For the protection and well being of your charges then, it behoves all aviculturists to give some serious thought to their possible theft or release. Birds, in an aviary, in a back yard or garden are extremely vulnerable. Many collections worth many thousands of dollars are frequently left unprotected nearly all day every day. The only thing separating the birds from the thief is a thin, easily and silently cut piece of wire. Yet the owner of these valuable birds would no more leave the family lawnmower on the front lawn, unprotected, than he would fly. No wonder then that these collections are increasingly being stolen. After giving a great deal of consideration to this matter over my own collection, I believe there are three main ways to overcome the problem, all will do so to varying degrees.

Suggestions to overcome a security problem

Firstly, a low profile. The less people who actually know one has a large bird collection or where one actually lives the better.

Secondly, staying at home. I know this sounds absolutely ludicrous but some aviculturists that own valuable birds are now doing just that. One or more members of the family stay at home simply to prevent intruders, well meaning or otherwise from entering their property in areas where they are not invited. Baby sitters are called in when there is nobody available within the family to stay at home. Crazy you may think, but not so to some of us that virtually eat, drink, think and live birds.

Thirdly, guard dogs. Dogs have been used for many years by many bird keepers to protect not only their birds but other belongings as well. Even if the dogs are not savage but continually bark at intruders, it will be enough to send most would-be-thieves scurrying as well as alerting informed neighbours. Dogs like geese, can only be regarded as a deterent or an early alarm.

Legal problems can arise from injuries caused by dogs even if intruders are the victims. Dogs will not stop a determined thief.

Next, alarm systems. There are a few different types on the market that can be applied to our bird keeping situation. There are those that detect heat (a persons body), or those that detect the movement of anything that is larger than a cat or small dog.

Other alarms are set off by an invisible light beam being broken or a pressure pad being stepped on. The costs of these alarms varies and will depend greatly on the area to be covered as well as the distance from your house etc. It is a cost though that is worth its weight in gold, as anyone that has experienced a theft will tell you. Concentrate on alarming the area around your aviaries. It is much better to be aware of approaching intruders before they have cut any wire or frightened any birds to death.

Finally, identify the birds. Tatoos, dyes or the more modern silicon chip can help return stolen birds to their rightful owners.

The Species

KEVIN WILSON

Crimson-winged Parrot
Princess Parrot
Regent Parrot
Superb Parrot
King Parrot
Red-capped Parrot
Mallee Ringnecked Parrot
Cloncurry Parrot
Port Lincoln Parrot
Twenty-eight Parrot
Red-fronted Kakariki
Yellow-fronted Kakariki

Crimson-winged Parrot

Aprosmictus erythropterus

Other Names: *Red-winged Parrot, Red-winged Lory, Blood-winged Parrot.*

Male

The head and neck of the Crimson-wing is bright apple green with its lower parts being slightly duller. The mantle is shiny black and the wing coverts sport a large, beautiful crimson patch. The rump is a deep ultramarine blue. The upper tail coverts are yellowish-green with tail feathers dark green tipped with a wash of pale yellowish-green. The bill is carroty-red with a yellow tip; eyes brown-red.
Length: 32cm.

Female

Overall a slightly duller shade of apple-green and a lighter blue rump. She lacks the black mantle of the male and the crimson red on the wings is limited to the outer wing coverts. Tail feathers green; bill pale orange; eyes dark brown.

Sexing

Sexing adults is no problem as they are so markedly dimorphic.
However, all young birds resemble the adult hen extremely closely, apart from the extreme tips of their tails showing rather more salmon pink than yellow. When young birds have attained seventeen or eighteen months of age, a few black feathers will begin to appear on the mantles of males and/or a few red feathers coming through on the wing coverts. Until then, the only guide as to sex is their behaviour; young males tend to be a little more aggressive when in the company of other birds. If they show their dominance by "telling off" or chortling to other birds, they are most likely males, as females are very meek and gentle creatures towards other birds. Crimson-wings attain their full, brilliant colour in their third year.

General

The striking brilliance of the male Crimson-wing with his resplendent red wings set against the shiny black back and glowing apple-green body, makes it one of the most attractive aviary birds. It isn't though, as popular in aviculture as its closest Australian relative, the King Parrot *Alisterus scapularis.* Its popularity may well have been appreciated more in Europe where it was kept and bred as early as 1881, whereas the first official breeding in Australia was in 1935.
Males can be remarkably pugnacious towards their mates or any other aviary inhabitant. The wisest course would be to house them just one pair per aviary. They are very strong flyers and require a flight of at least five metres (16ft 8in) in length, one metre (3ft 4in) wide and at least two metres (6ft 8in) high, higher if possible. Generally they are quite timid birds and when their aviary is entered, will fly madly from one end to the other emitting loud screeching calls. If there is sufficient area above their keeper's head for them to fly, I'm sure they will be much less likely

to collide with anything. Because they are such a nervous bird in captivity, I believe they would make better, steadier more easily cared for and bred birds if they were hand raised. In my own experience, birds that have been hand raised and placed in an aviary soon after weaning make much better avicultural subjects. Firstly because, as stated they are steadier and don't display wild and erratic behaviour when approached and secondly they seem to be less easily put off when parenting young and having their nests inspected.

Crimson-wings are notorious for dying not long after they have been newly purchased. Even though plenty of the most nourishing and tasty food is offered they decline to eat and very soon waste away to mere skin and bone before dropping dead. In an effort to alleviate this problem, many bird keepers do what they can to treat these "sick" birds, taking them to the vet and/ or dosing them up with medicines. All this I fear, to the bird's further detriment. I am convinced that with Crimson-wings we should be dealing with their mental outlook as much as their physical outlook. Most trapped birds inevitably end up dead as their natural fear and timidity bring about this consequence. Extreme care and empathy should be given to newly acquired birds until they are fully settled. Hand raised Crimson-wings tend to be much more stress resistent and will cope with any moves without dramas.

Once they are settled they are no problem at all, they do not usually chew the woodwork of an aviary and are not hostile towards their neighbours. I have found them to be hardy in the extreme, enjoying the full heat of summer whilst tolerating, without ill effects, the extremities of icy and snowy winters. Because they are basically arboreal, they enjoy a fresh branch of Eucalypt each day, attacking leaf tips and buds with great fervour. The late Duke of Bedford also enjoyed this bird's attributes a he penned: "For the combined virtues of gorgeous loveliness, all round hardiness, non destructiveness to the fabric of the aviary, simple requirements, and regular, if not exceedingly prolific breeding, the Crimson-wing comes first among all the large parakeets I have kept".

These birds usually ignore a bowl of water given them for bathing, rather,they favour hanging on the wire and flapping their wings in the rain. The only time I have seen them go to the ground is to use a ground based water bowl. I therefore think that they are more comfortable staying up higher and their food and water receptacles are accordingly placed up high.

Breeding

Hens can be sexually mature at just twelve months of age while cocks are incapable of fertilising eggs until they are fully coloured, in their third year. If a cock and hen have been together since young, compatibility shouldn't be a problem. If however, adult birds are put together, care has to be taken. Males are renowned for their hostile attitude towards females at the best of times, but when an unknown female is placed in his presence, then all hell may break loose. She could be hounded by him to the point of complete exhaustion. He is better placed in her aviary where she is more familiar and perhaps more able to stand her ground for her own territory. If his aggression continues, a clipped wing could cool his heels.

When they do settle down, his disposition towards her may never be more than a spiteful tolerance, certainly not one of a devoted husband. Nevertheless they do manage to conjoin long enough to breed. This is proceeded by a virtually nondescript mating display. The male displays to his female quivering his wings and blazing his eyes while dancing around her from side to side. This performance is interspersed with his flitting from one end of the aviary to the other emitting a noisy metallic note. He carries on with this for about two weeks whereupon he begins to peer into the log or box every now and then. About this time the female is starting also to inspect the log and give long whining calls in a lowered, crouching posture begging to be fed.

1 - WILSON MOORE

1 - A large log to ground level has often proved successful in the breeding of Crimson-wings and King Parrots.

A long hollow log or a grandfather type box should be offered them, although after establishing themselves as parents they will often accept nests shorter than their counterparts in the wild. 1.5 to 2 metres (5-6ft 8in) should be long enough with an inside diameter of about 20 to 25cm (8-10in). It needs to be angled slightly and if a man-made box, a metal ladder fixed or wooden rungs glued in place to make access and departure easier for the hen. Crimson-wings have a habit of laying eggs and sometimes even rearing young on the floor of the aviary. (The cardboard box method as discussed under King Parrots may be of some help in these cases). Wild birds will from time to time, after entering the nest hole, descend as much as 9 or 10 metres (30-33ft) to the nesting chamber, nearly down to ground level. This would strongly indicate that they favour these 'near the ground' nests. Positioning a long log or box barely off or on the ground has achieved a great deal of success in the past with pairs that have otherwise not accepted a given nest.

The breeding season of Crimson-wings in captivity lasts from September to December when the hen will incubate between three and six eggs, usually three, for between nineteen and twenty one days. When the chicks hatch they are covered in a thick white down which is replaced by a grey down in about ten to twelve days. Although reluctant to feed the incubating hen he will take an increased share in the feeding duties while the young are being reared. When the young are about six weeks old they fledge. During this rearing period, caution needs to be exercised when inspections are deemed necessary as some hens will abandon the nest for some time or even desert their young altogether if the disturbance is too great.

Mutations

The only known mutation in Crimson-wings is a yellow variety in Europe and a 'mostly' yellow type often referred to as Cinnamon here in Australia.

Hybrids

This species has hybridised with Australian King, Superb, Princess, Regent and the Sula Island King Parrot.

1 - Cock Crimson-wing.
2 - Hen Crimson-wing
Parrots are also
beautiful with only a
little less brilliance.
3 - Magnificent in its
beauty the cock
Crimson-wing makes a
wonderful aviary
subject.

Princess Parrot

Polytelis alexandrae

Other Names : Princess of Wales Parakeet, Alexandra Parakeet, Princess Alexandra's Parakeet, Queen Alexandra's Parakeet, Alexandrine, Spinifex Parrot, Rose-throated Parrot.

Male

Crown and forehead blue-grey; neck and back olive-green; chest greyish-green; wing coverts yellowish-green; primaries dull blue with an elongated spatule on the third primary; throat, foreneck, thighs and lower flanks rose pink; lower back and rump blue-grey; extremely long central tail feathers (sometimes more than half the overall length of the bird) olive green; outer tail feathers blue-grey with pink inner webs; bill bright coral pink.
Length: 45cm.

Female

Females are similar in overall colouration at first glance. A closer inspection will reveal some small distinguishing features.

Firstly the shading on the females crown and forehead tends to be a little less bright than the male and more greyish-mauve. The rump too is a duller blue-grey. Most females have shorter tails but not always so. Some older hens have tails that are as equally as long as some males.

Sexing

Immature birds look like females only slightly duller and with shorter tails. Some males exhibit larger, flatter, more brightly coloured heads. If a young bird begins to chortle, chuckle and raise the crest feathers on its head in display, it will certainly be a male. This display is often carried out at just a few months of age and is a definite determination of sex. As young Princess grow, the male's coral pink bill also becomes brighter as does the blue on his crown and rump. From about twelve months of age, males develop a peculiar spatule or feather protrudence, sometimes growing to 20mm (1in) long on the tip of each of the third primaries. At this age there is no difficulty in sexing Princess Parrots.

The Princess Parrot has always been a very desirable aviary specimen, these beautiful pastel shaded birds are considered a prize in even the most avid aviculturists collection. Apart from their pleasing colours their long, graceful shape also adds to their desirability, but even this is by far surpassed by its enchanting and friendly character.

Even if not to begin with these charming birds soon become very tame with their friendly personality shining through. The bird's confidence in its keeper is demonstrated when visiting them each morning and evening. My birds love to clamber all over one another in an effort to get to the fruit and vegetables that have been brought for them. They do not mind running over your hands or even a brief hop from your shoulder or head en route to the food. If you were to wait long enough they would eventually regard you as a fixture solely placed there for their own delight. They will not hesitate to dance and bob all over you happily chuckling their contented notes. If you appear to be giving one bird more attention than the other, it will become quite "cranky" at its mate and insist that it too receives more consideration. The famous bird keeper, the Duke of Bedford, was obviously besotted by their captivating behaviour as he wrote of them: "No parakeet is naturally so fearless of mankind nor so easily tamed and, while it dislikes being touched and handled, as do all species which have not the habit of caressing their mates, none is more delighted by being spoken to and noticed by its owner and none will give him a devotion more free of cupboard love. Almost any Princess of Wales will come up and display if you cluck and chirrup to him for a few minutes and tell him he is a pretty bird. Aviary bred young, instead of being desperately timid, will be sitting on your arm and feeding before other young parakeets will even be reasonably steady....." I must state at this point that, if you have these birds housed in an aviary that does not have a safety porch or corridor, be extremely careful that you do not exit your cage with one of these birds perched, unbeknown to you, on your back. No matter how tame they become, your chances of retrieving an escapee may be limited.

Princess Parrots in the wild state are nomadic birds that enjoy many thousands of square kilometres and, although obviously not feasible to give even a recognisable percentage of that great open space, need as much space as is reasonably possible. If housed in single pairs rather than on the colony system the minimum aviary size should be no less than 3.6m (12ft) hopefully much more. When more are housed together a much larger aviary is needed. Only in such a cage can the beauty of their long tapering tail be appreciated as they fly from perch to perch. Not only does it trail with an elegant upward sweep but very often fans out displaying that attractive, radiant pink underside for all to see.

Material selected for your aviary construction may be determined by either your budget or your existing setup. As long as the aviary is well constructed with adequate shelter from bad weather and is at least two metres high it will be suitable for Princess.

They are not wood chewers and can be held without fear of escape behind even chicken wire. However having said that, a stronger wire would be advisable to keep out unwanted intruders that may be able to damage a very light gauge wire, such as other wild parrots, cats or dogs.

There are probably very few, if any places within Australia that could be considered inhospitable to these birds. They are kept and bred in all climates with no apparent ill effects, that is of course providing they are given adequate protection. My own birds can be seen each winter pecking about on the snow-laden floors of their aviaries and, in Europe they also fare well and breed under extremely cold conditions. On those very hot summer days they enjoy a shower from the hose set in the spray mode. They will hang on the wire or from the ceiling flaying their wings in all directions in an effort to catch as many cooling droplets as they can. When the shower is over, they will sometimes sit for an hour preening every feather on their body. It's a delight to watch.

These birds tend to spend much of the day sitting with their

1 - Princess hen.
2 - Princess cock.
3 - Princess hen.

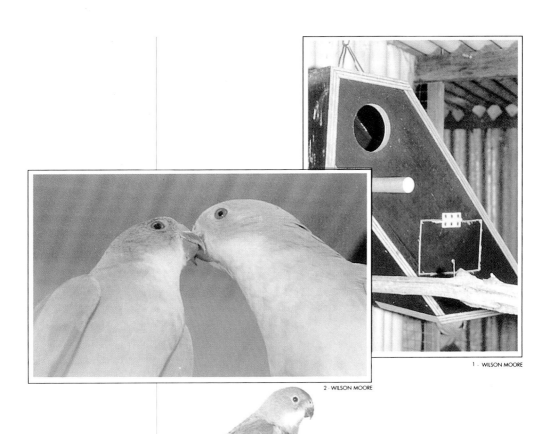

1 - WILSON MOORE

2 - WILSON MOORE

3 - PETER ODEKERKIN

4 - WILSON MOORE

1 - A successful
nesting box design for
Princess. The sloping
box prevents the hen
jumping straight down
on her eggs.
2 - The cook on right
feeds his hen while
dilating and
contracting his pupils
during courtship.
3 - Blue Princess
4 - The Blue Princess
has many admirers.

Page 43

heads tucked over their shoulder and looking "fluffed up." Only careful observation will eventually enable you to distinguish between this posture and the behaviour of a bird that is chilled or otherwise ill.

Because they spend a great deal of time scavenging on the floor of the aviary, they are prone to worm infestation and therefore need to be de-wormed regularly. Intestinal worms are probably the single most causative agent in the death of Princess Parrots. Birds will often look completely healthy right up to the moment they drop dead.

Many aviculturists house Princess Parrots with Neophema species (Bourkes, Scarlet-chested, Turquoisines, Blue-wings and Elegants) because of their placid nature. Others have shared their home with a pair or two of finches. In most cases all get along quite well, however it has been noted that breeding results are not optimum. This is probably because there exists, albeit small, some mild animosity between the species when nesting.

Breeding

In their wild state Princess Parrots are nomadic and breed according to the rains and subsequent availability of seeding grasses which can be at any time of the year. In captivity the breeding season begins approximately (depending on locality) in August through to December.

Birds as young as one year old may wish to go to nest but, generally their efforts are wasted. They are often very eager to begin with but may peter out, deserting the eggs or young or just breaking the eggs before they even hatch. All this is of course due to their inexperience and they will normally do better the second year round. Some breeders prevent them from breeding in their first year by removing nesting boxes or logs from their aviary to avoid the disappointment of lost eggs or young. I, on the other hand let them try if they wish, sometimes with marvelous results, other times, as I say, disappointment. I use nest boxes that are about 20cm (8in) x 20cm (8in) and 45cm (18in) tall. Other sizes though, larger and smaller have been accepted and also work well. The entrance hole is about 8cm (3in) wide and has a natural log spout that is glued around the hole. This gives them something to land on and alight from when entering or leaving the nest. The nesting receptacles ideally should always incorporate an inspection door, a sliding plate on the top or a hinged door cut into the side. I prefer the door in the side as this means I do not have to remove the box or log or stand on a box or ladder to peer down from the top. The base of the nest is covered with a compact mixture of peat moss and wood shavings and if a nest box is being used, wooden slats or a wire ladder is fixed on one side leading to the exit hole. Natural logs, unless excessively smooth do not need these refinements. These "steps" leading to the base of the nesting chamber are very important with Princess as they have a habit of wanting to drop straight down onto and breaking the eggs. Some birds even though they have a ladder will still insist on jumping on the eggs. This can be overcome by placing the box or log on an angle sufficient to force the bird to walk down the side to the eggs. Care must be taken when young ones are near fledging as they may leave the nest too soon, the exit being too easy to reach.

Another problem encountered by some breeders is egg

eating. There has been no, one hundred percent effective method of preventing this. However some success has been achieved by placing smooth, white pebbles of a similar size to the eggs in the nest. When the parent birds find they cannot bite through these "eggs" they give up.

Mating is pre-empted by often long periods of courtship displays and an incessant ringing of a single note call. The male will make this call when in flight or when perched, raising his head with an upward motion with each whistle. Only the male makes this piping call which will often last for hours. After his elaborate courtship display which may also include head bobbing, swiftly wiping his beak, eyes blazing and "running on the spot" a clicking noise will emanate from his throat. She will solicit food when ready to accept his amorous advances.

Princess Parrots are also one of the few Australian species that can be bred on the colony system, that is more than one pair per flight. Colonies as large as fifty birds have been known. The size of the colony depends, of course, on the size of the aviary that they are housed in. Plenty of logs and boxes should be offered and if at all possible all the occupants should be placed in the aviary at the same time to prevent any territorial squabbling. It is debatable whether breeding successes are greater or lesser in a colony system, some breeders have remarkable success while others have achieved little or none at all and yet do well when their birds are housed in single pairs.

You can expect between four to six eggs to be laid with only the hen incubating them. After about nineteen to twenty one days the eggs will hatch and the young will be ready to leave the nest in about another six weeks. The male feeds the female while in the nest and will also share in feeding the young when they fledge until they wean. If the young are taken from the nest within the first two weeks to be hand raised, the pair will almost certainly nest again. Some birds will nest again even after raising the first clutch for the season. A second nest box may be hung in place as she may lay her second batch of eggs before her first clutch have fledged. If only one clutch is reared the young can be left in all safety with the parents even after they become fully independent.

Occasionally, males will want to share the nesting chamber while the hen is incubating eggs, a habit to be discouraged. Broken eggs have resulted from this bad habit. If it is seen to occur, the male should be removed from the aviary till the eggs have hatched where upon he will commence feeding the hen.

Mutations

The first mutation to occur in the Princess Parrot was the Blue. As with most blue mutations it is a very pleasing shade of blue and grey. The normally pink areas on the bird are replaced with white. This mutation is an Australian original, it first appeared in the aviaries of Mr George Ruddle of South Australia in 1951. Since then they have occurred in aviaries in Europe and America. The Blue is recessive in its genetic inheritance therefore both cocks and hens can be split for Blue.

The next to arrive on the scene was the spectacular Lutino, it is without doubt one of the rarest mutations in this country.

Interestingly, it had its beginnings in, of all places, East Germany in the mid 1970s (two hens). Sadly, the only way for this beautiful mutation to get into the hands of breeders in the west, was to have it smuggled across the border. In 1978 a West German breeder managed to smuggle them into northern Germany and is now increasing their numbers. The bird is overall bright yellow with a white belly. The pink on the throat, legs and tail are retained, contrasting nicely with the yellow. (Lutino never masks red). Its eyes are red.

Both the Blue and the Lutino are autosomal recessive and when paired will give offspring that are double split (split Blue and Lutino). Double split paired to double split will result in nine different possibilities, of which one of those nine is Albino. Thus the Albino is alive, well and being bred, albeit in few numbers only at the moment.

A Red Princess is currently being developed in Australia and I have seen a variety of birds whose colour vary from a barely noticeable difference to that of a stunning, wine coloured bird that has nearly all of its green feathers replaced with red ones.

Whether this is true mutation or brought about by selective breeding ie. reddest cock to reddest hen, remains to be seen.

Hybrids

Princess Parrots have been hybridised with the Superb *Polytelis swainsonii*, Regent *P. anthopeplus*, Crimson-wing *Aprosmictus erythropterus* and the Indian Ringneck *Psittacula krameri*.

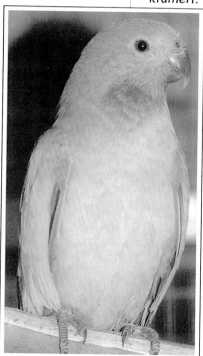

1 - WILSON MOORE

2 - CURRUMBIN SANCTUARY

3 - CURRUMBIN SANCTUARY

1 - *Cock Princess.*
2 - *Princess are generally devoted parents. These chicks are still being fed while their box is cleaned out.*
3 - *Three Princess chicks 15 days old and one 12 days old.*

Regent Parrot

Polytelis anthopeplus

Other Names: Rock Pebbler, Rock Peplar, Rockies, Smoker, Black-tailed Parrot, Marlock Parrot.

Male

Overall body colour varies in different specimens from daffodil yellow in the eastern form (parts of N.S.W., S.A. and Victoria), to greenish yellow in the western form (W.A.). Mantle, crown and hind neck olive green; wings mostly yellow with primaries and secondaries black and a broad band of carmine-red across the inner wing coverts; tail feathers are black; eyes orange-brown; bill coral-red.

Length: 41cm.

Female

Female Regents are almost entirely olive-green, the carmine-red flash on the inner wing coverts being a little duller; underneath the bronze-green tail she sports pink tipped feathers. The bill is a duller coral.

Sexing

To the untrained eye young Regents can be almost impossible to sex. Some young males exhibit a richer yellow though, even while in the nest. As they grow, when about six or eight months old the deeper yellow in males becomes clearly evident about the head and chest. Adult plumage, but not yet the richest yellow, is reached at about eighteen months. The deepest yellow shows after at least two years. Not unlike Princess Parrots, young males will burble and chortle away happily for hours, giving away their male identity.

General

Regent Parrots, although not the gaudiest of parrots could certainly be called one of the most pleasingly coloured and one of the friendliest. They make an excellent inmate for our aviaries having no serious or nasty traits at all. Even when adult birds are purchased they soon become quite tame and will hungrily eat from your hand. Young birds raised in the aviary tend to be naturally tame, taking every opportunity to land directly on your head or shoulder when you enter their home. The only aggression they seem to offer is out of jealousy, if one youngster has the prime position on your arm and another wants it, both birds bodies are stretched out with heads held high and beaks open emanating a threatening vocal barrage to one another but never actually coming to blows.

Because they are such a placid bird they can be housed with other non-aggressive species, except perhaps finches. Their amusing nature allows them to playfully destroy the finches' nests, pulling them apart strand by strand to the bewilderment and utter abhorrence of the finches. In more cases than most they are amiably housed with parrots of the Neophema variety. I have never known them to attack the aviary woodwork to any harmful degree and need no stronger gauge wire than chicken wire. A heavier gauge wire, if used would give more protection though for the birds from such predators as hawks, falcons, dogs and cats. To coop these beautiful birds in an aviary that is too small would neither bring out the best in their joyful nature or their breeding abilities. At least 4m (13ft 4in) long and 1m (3ft 4in) wide with a height of 2m (6ft 8in) should be provided for their needs but I'm certain they would be even happier in something nearing 5m or 6m (16ft 8in - 20ft) long. The bigger the better. Keep in mind also that just because these birds are amiable and make good mixers, they should not be deprived of space by having too many birds in an aviary that is really only suitable for perhaps one or two pairs. I was once told of a horrendous number of birds being kept in a relatively small aviary. With great pride a bird keeper told me how he had pairs of Kings, Princess, Regents, Superbs, Bourkes, Red-rumps and Rainbow Lorikeets all housed in an aviary that measured 4m (13ft 4in) x 3.5m (11ft 8in). This misguided person that kept these birds was absolutely amazed that none of his birds would breed for him. I was quite amazed that any of his birds were still alive to even consider breeding. Regent Parrots cannot, by any stretch of the imagination be called proficient flyers in a confined space, and therefore need as much room as you can offer them for their contentment and well being.

As far as noise is concerned, even neighbours with exceptionally acute hearing could find no cause for complaint. Perhaps the noisiest they ever get is when they are breeding but even that is really of no consequence and a neighbour that complains about that amount of noise obviously doesn't like you.

The Regent Parrot is a hardy bird that can be kept in outside aviaries the length and breadth of Australia. Care and attention needs to be given though, to adequate protection from inclement weather. Damp weather and a cool breeze is a certain recipe for killing birds, so make sure that they have proper housing to protect them. If in a warm climate, they will appreciate the cooling droplets of a fine spray from the garden hose, clinging open winged from the aviary wire in an effort to catch every drop they can. Once completely saturated, they will sit for the next hour or so drying off and preening their newly cleaned feathers.

Spraying them once in a while is quite necessary in periods of no rain for them to maintain good plumage. Curiously, even if given a wide bowl of water in which to bath, they won't. On the other hand if housed in an area prone to ice and snow, as long as they have dry and protected quarters, they will thrive, even paddling in the snow on the ground searching out a morsel to eat.

There are two important things to watch for with Regent Parrots; Firstly, intestinal worms. Because they do spend so much time on the ground fossicking for food they are apt to contaminate and re-contaminate themselves continually. A good drench directly to the crop three or four times per year keeps them clear of infestation. Secondly, Regents, although apparently in good health can be carriers of microplasmosis which, when a bird is under severe stress is evident in the form of chronic conjunctivitis. Some strains of this eye problem respond to treatment, others do not. In all cases of this nature however, the wisest thing to do would be to consult your nearest avian vet.

Of the three members belonging to the Polytelis genus, the

Regent is the largest. The other members are the Princess Parrot *P.alexandrae*, and the Superb Parrot *P. swainsonii*.

Breeding

Regent Parrots are not considered difficult to breed, having been bred in Australia as far back as 1865 and in Europe since 1880.

Providing one gives them proper conditions and a suitable diet, there is no reason why most healthy birds will not breed for their owners, even newcomers to bird keeping.

The whole breeding process begins between August and November with a cock that is at least two years old and a hen that is at least of a similar age, although some hens will rear young successfully from only twelve months. For about two weeks prior to her entering the nest, she will pester him to be fed, persistently crying in an effort to get his attention. He though, is a reluctant lover in most cases, and needs every bit of encouragement to feed her. This, when accomplished, sparks off investigation of the log or box in expectation of egg laying. Interestingly though, the female of one of my pairs, after about two weeks of begging, failed to enter the nest box. The male for the next two weeks chased her mercilessly in an effort to get her into the box. Quite unusual really when you consider the female is the dominant one in this species. He was so persistent at times that I thought that he was going to do her an injury so I caught him up and clipped one of his wings, just enough to inhibit his flight somewhat and cool his ardour. Eventually she did enter the box and laid five eggs. Four or five is the usual amount laid, but in seasons when all of my birds seem to lay smaller clutches, they have laid just two or three eggs, all being fertile.

Either man made boxes or natural logs can be used as Regents do not seem to be too fussy. Where I can I'll use a man made nest box over a natural log as each and every log we use for captive breeding probably takes away a nest site from birds in the wild.

All those hundreds of logs we see at bird dealers all have to come from somewhere, and it really is getting more and more difficult for some species to find good nesting hollows in the wild as many of the choicest are taken, in some areas, for the bird trade. I use boxes measuring approximately 60cm (2ft) long and 26cm (10in) wide and 26cm (10in) deep. The entrance hole has a hollow, small log tube that is about 10cm (4in) in diameter and about 15cm (6in) long. I have found these entrance tubes to be very successful with many species, perhaps it's because it makes the nest a little darker inside. The hen enjoys just sitting in this small hollow with just her head peering out, ready at any disturbance to retreat to the safety it gives her, without having to completely drop into the nesting chamber. In the side of the box, near the base, is a little hinged door just large enough to get my hand in if need be. Having this inspection door on the side means I never have to lift the box down from the aviary wall, thus making any checks quick and hassle free for both me and the birds. Most breeders have their own nesting material formula, mine is very easily put together. It is simply 50% sawdust and 50% peat moss,available at any garden centre. I have read that some breeders like to dampen this mixture when placed into the box, but I cannot see any benefit in this as, if the weather is warm, by the time the bird starts to actually sit on it, it will have dried out

1 - PETER ODEKERKIN

2 - KEVIN WILSON

4 - WILSON MOORE

3 - PETER ODEKERKIN

1 - Regent cock.
2 - Regent cock.
3 - Regent hen.
4 - Pair of Regents.
Cock on right.

1 - PETER ODEKERKIN

2 - WILSON MOORE

3 - WILSON MOORE

5 - KEVIN WILSON

4 - KEVIN WILSON

1 - Regent chick 32 days old.
2 - Hen Regent.
3 - Cock Regent.
4 - Regent hen at her nest.
5 - Hand-reared Regents can make beautiful pets.

anyway. As long as they have plenty of access to fresh, clean water they can keep the box humid by themselves, naturally.

Exact incubation time has eluded me. In Ian Harman's book Australian Parrots in Bush and Aviary, he says twenty three days, as does Hutchinson and Lovell in Australian Parrots - A field and Aviary Study. But George Smith in Lovebirds and Related Parrots and Rosemary Low's Parrot's their care and Breeding both give the time as nineteen days. Forshaw does not comment at all on the Regents incubation time. To find out for myself I decided to keep a very accurate record of their breeding behaviour. While I commend the accurate keeping of records in aviculture, I have learnt a quick lesson with Regents in my possession. I have three pairs of the yellow form; the first I inspected regularly and when the five eggs were about one week old they were abandoned.

The second pair raised chicks to almost one week with only periodical inspection and then the parents abandoned them. The third pair, after the preceding mishaps, were left entirely on their own and happily raised three healthy young until about one month old, when severe cold winds for nearly four days "chilled" mother, and she had to be placed in a hospital cage for a couple of days to recuperate. The unusually cold, windy weather along with the strain of raising three growing chicks, was just too much for her. Happily though, she recovered and the three chicks were fed by hand. All are now in good health and the three young being as tame and friendly as only those that have hand raised could realise. One could strongly be tempted to keep them as pets when so tame, but I think it better for the birds to be in an aviary than a small cage, though the late Duke of Bedford wrote of the Regent Parrot as a pet:- "Young birds are easily tamed and make attractive pets, becoming very sociable and possessing some powers of mimicry. A cock in my possession whistles the tune 'Yes we have no bananas' right through, and tries to talk in a hoarse, inZdistinctive voice. Another in the possession of a friend imitates perfectly the cooing of a dove, the natural cry of this parrot is almost impossible to describe in print; as parakeet calls go, it is not unduly loud or unpleasant." The young fledge at about five weeks of age and are independent in a further two or three weeks. I have found soft food and soaked seed is an invaluable aid to weaning.

Mutations

A rare yellow-backed variety has been developed in Europe but very little is known about it.

In Australia a Red Regent has been available in extremely small numbers. Individual birds vary in the amount of wine-red colour covering their plumage. I have seen a very good example of one that was, even though a little patchy, covered almost entirely in this deep, rich shade of red.

Hybrids

Regent Parrots have hybridised with the Princess Parrot P. alexandrae, the Superb Parrot P. swainsonii and the Crimson-winged Parrot Aprosmictus erythropterus.

Superb Parrot

Polytelis swainsonii

Other Names: *Barraband, Green Leek, Scarlet-breasted Parrot.*

Male

Overall body and wings bright, light green; forepart of head, throat and cheeks canary yellow; immediately beneath the yellow on his foreneck is a broad crescent of crimson red; bend of wings, blue; tail upper surface grass green, underneath black; bill light coral-red, eyes yellow-orange.
Length: 41cm.

Female

Adult females are a slightly duller green than the male and lack both the brilliant yellow on the head and face as well as the red crescent. She does however usually have a few flecks of red on the thigh feathers and also has a bluish tinge, faint but discernible, on her cheeks. The underside of her tail feathers, except the central pair, have pink tips. Her eyes are yellow.

Sexing

Immature Superbs can be extremely difficult to sex, they tend to resemble females but lack the giveaway bluish tinge to the cheeks. All youngsters carry the pink tips to the underside of the tail feathers, males eventually moult this out. Some of them, both male and female, have a few red feathers about the thighs, so this is not a good indication to sex. Males will reveal a brighter shade of green when held in good light, but this can still be difficult for those with an untrained eye, especially if you have a nest full of either cocks or hens. Males may start to develop some red or yellow feathers about the throat and neck anywhere from three months on up to sometimes the third year.

Normally though, adult plumage is attained at about fifteen to eighteen months. The only reliable indication to sexing young birds is the more active behaviour and chortling of males.

General

Although the Superb Parrot is probably the most brilliantly coloured of the three polytelids, it seems to be the least popular. Exactly why this is I am not sure. This magnificent parrot has everything going for it to make it such a good choice for either the budding aviculturist or the more advanced. Much like the Princess and the Regent, it has a very pleasing, docile and inoffensive nature. It takes remarkably little time for any newly acquired adult birds to build a great deal of adoration for their keeper. Whistling, chirruping and softly talking to them, as well as offering them tid-bits of fresh seeding grasses will soon have them clinging to the wire at face level responding in kind to win over your affections. Their charm is further enhanced by their natural ability to mimic other birds and even, to a lesser degree, the human voice.

Their aviary may be constructed of wood as they are not prone to chewing its structure. However, when bunches of

1 - KEVIN WILSON

3 - KEVIN WILSON

2 - KEVIN WILSON

1 - Hen Superb.
2 - Hen Superb.
3 - Pair of Superb
Parrots.

Page 54

1 - The striking yellow face and red throat band contrasts the solid green body colour of the cock Superb.
2 - Cock Superb.
3 - Superb Parrot chicks 7, 8, 10 and 11 days old.
4 - Superb chicks, from right, 14, 15, 17 and 18 days old.

Eucalypts are offered to them, especially if flowering, they will spend many enjoyable hours chewing on them and stripping them of their leaves and eagerly consuming the pollen and nectar from the flowers, which they also delight in eating. In their natural habitat they tend to live and breed in the stands of Eucalypts that border water courses, so this provision of leafy branches probably goes a long way to making them feel "at home".

The sweet nature of Superbs also means they can be housed safely with other species; they are particularly suited to the Neophema species but will also dwell quite amiably alongside Cockatiels and King Parrots. Although they have been bred in such mixed company, they are more likely to reproduce when in an aviary of their own.

Superbs are naturally a sociable bird, even when breeding they tend to flock in relatively large groups, yet when breeding in captivity, aviculturists have had little success when attempting to breed them in a colony. I have found that they are more successful when housed just one pair to a flight, but within sight of other pairs. A single pair can be very difficult to encourage to go down, but others in the near vicinity seem to act as a stimulant. As a general rule Superbs are mostly kept in aviaries around 4m (13ft 4in) to 6m (20ft) long and perhaps a metre or two wide, and this seems to be fine for a single pair.

However, if they were to be housed in something much larger, say ten times larger than this, I am confident the colony system of breeding would work extremely well.

Even though I have never personally experienced either problem with any of my own Superbs, there are two enigmas that seem to frequently befall these birds. The first and probably most common is a form of conjunctivitis. It appears to be an ailment that can be quite difficult to cure if not dealt with straight away. Although, after speaking with fellow aviculturists, I have been led to believe that, in most cases, the remedies tried have either been home-spun or prescribed by vets who admittedly have very little knowledge of avian diseases. Obviously, it would be prudent on behalf of those keeping Superbs to familiarise themselves with the first sign of this problem. This is usually indicated by the bird rubbing it's eye on the perch or wire. An avian veterinarian will then likely be able to effect a cure.

More often than not it affects a single eye that it blinks continuously or may keep shut for longer than normal periods. Closer inspection of the eye will undoubtedly reveal a watery fluid covering the eyeball and may even be matting the surrounding feathers. The eyelids may also appear reddish and thicker than normal. If left, the eye will eventually "clag" together and become even more swollen. This condition is obviously uncomfortable for the bird which will be seen trying to wipe its eye over the perch in an effort to alleviate the discomfort. This, no doubt adds to the spreading of the disease.

If this problem arises, consult your avian vet immediately. To help prevent it spreading to the other occupants of the aviary, isolate the affected bird and change and burn the old perches.

A word of warning is appropriate here, eye trouble can be an early sign of Chlamydia. This disease will almost certainly kill your bird if left untreated for even a short period of time. Chlamydia requires a different treatment to conjunctivitis.

The second ailment that seems to befall this species, although less common, is leg paralysis. A condition where the toes curl up, sometimes extremely tightly and makes it impossible for the bird to perch, even though all other bodily functions appear to be normal, including flight. It appears to be more common in males and has been a problem that has existed since before these birds were trapped and shipped overseas more than thirty years ago. Importers would find otherwise healthy, cripples, amongst each shipment they received. As mentioned I have had no first-hand experience with this ailment, so I shall quote from British veterinarian and aviculturist George A. Smith's Lovebirds and Related Parrots on the subject: "Treatment has been as bizarre as suggesting that rubbing the legs with a mixture of glycerine and alcohol will improve the circulation of the blood; to a diet which is rich in protein; or to give a vitamin enriched drinking water. Autopsy has always revealed no abnormality to explain the paralysis. The fact that the paralysis occurs at a time when the males are most sexually aroused or under conditions of nervous stress and that a similar paralysis has been seen in a clutch of hand reared Rock Pebblers that suffered from a non-diagnosed yet, presumably contagious, nephritis indicates that the paralysis is brought on by pressure on, or inflammation of, the sciatic nerve." Some birds have recovered from this condition after a Vitamin B treatment.

Breeding

A prolific breeding pair of Superbs has been known to produce young for twenty years. Some people have virtually moved mountains in an effort to induce them to breed, still, with no satisfaction. Perhaps the best way to start, would be to buy two or three young pairs. Choose carefully as they are not the easiest bird to sex. Many aquaintances have voiced their disappointment when their birds have all, if not most, coloured up to be males (surgical sexing will remove any doubts). For some reason more cocks are produced than hens. If possible place these young birds in a flight together and let them choose their own mates well before they are fully coloured. When paired off, move them into separate flights, preferably in sight of each other. Then, while waiting for them to mature do your utmost in building and maintaining strong, healthy stock.

The breeding season begins in September and lasts till December. Nest boxes or logs need to be in place well before the season starts. 60cm (2ft) long and about 18cm (7in) square is suitable if using a man-made box and a little longer if a natural log is given. Many writers suggest that natural logs are preferred over boxes, but I have never found this to be so. My birds have readily accepted boxes that are hung on an acute angle, and in one case, even though they were nesting quite happily, their box was inadvertently "knocked" into an almost upright position, still, they cheerfully continued raising their family. As with most birds though, I suggest that two or more logs or boxes are positioned in the aviary, giving them every possible opportunity to go to nest. When they have selected a nest, the others can be removed. Like the Regent and Princess Parrots, the courtship can be quite elaborate. Sometimes well before breeding actually commences the male will raise his head feathers slightly, stare with contracted pupils at his mate and utter a twittering call while holding out and slightly drooping his wings. His ardour is further displayed by sometimes frantic running and flying around the hen. She, depending on her state of readiness will either ignore him and go about her normal everyday business or will be reproductively active and noisily solicit feeding. When he eventually responds to her soliciting, the mating begins.

The normal clutch laid is either four or five eggs and they are incubated by the hen for about twenty two days. If the eggs are inspected and found to be clear (infertile), they can be removed thus giving the hen a further chance to go down again. When the chicks hatch they are covered in a fluffy white down and for the first couple of weeks of their lives are rarely left by their mother. During the incubation and first couple of weeks rearing the young it is inadvisable to inspect the nest unless necessary as females are notoriously easily upset at this time. At four weeks of age it is a wonderful sight to see young Superbs coming to the entrance hole, just two or three heads popping out all clammering for dad to feed them.

In another week or so they will be ready to test their own wings and this they sometimes do with horrendous consequences. Their flight can be so erratic and uncontrolled that they often smash headlong into the aviary wall or wire. Until they have mastered their flight a little better, usually within the week, their keepers should move about their flight with extreme care, slowly and steadily.

Mutations

Apart from the skin of a Lutino Superb Parrot held in the Australian museum in Sydney, there are no other recorded mutations.

Hybrids

Superbs have hybridised with Princess, Regents, Crimsonwings and Australian King Parrots.

1 - Hen Superb.

1 - KEVIN WILSON

King Parrot

Alisterus scapularis

Other Names: *Australian King, Eastern King, Queensland King, King Lory, Scarlet Parrot, Green Parrot.*

Male

Head, neck, chest and abdomen bright scarlet; mantle, back and wings are dark green; on the hind neck separating red from green is a narrow band of dark blue; lower back and rump dark blue; wing coverts carry a longitudinal pale green stripe; upper tail coverts blue-black; central tail feathers black; upper mandible black with a red tip, lower mandible black, his eyes are yellow.
Length: 43cm.

Female

Overall colouration is basically green with the upper neck suffused with dull red; lower breast and abdomen scarlet red; rump blue green; central tail feathers green; lateral feathers green-blue. Most females do not carry the pale green wing stripe but where they have been recorded they are less prominent than the male's. The bill is black and her eyes are pale yellow.

Sexing

Immature Kings look like adult hens but have paler greyish coloured bills. When approaching six months of age the bills of young males begin to turn reddish. As they reach twelve months (the first moult) a few red feathers appear on the head and upper chest of males.

General

The King Parrot would undoubtedly be one of Australia's most recognisable parrots, especially along the east coast where it inhabits the dense woods and forests from as far as the mid north coast of Queensland down to southern Victoria. In spite of their vivacious colouring, Kings are definitely one of those birds that appear not to be fully appreciated by Australian aviculturists.

This is borne out by the fact that not a great many Kings are bred in Australian aviaries. Unfortunately, many an unsuspecting aviculturist has bought parrots that sadly have been taken from the wild. Overseas they are very highly sought after, not only because of their brilliant colours but also because when suitably housed they make extremely attractive and acrobatic aviary subjects. King Parrots exude a joie de vivre that is second to none and they exhibit this freely by their bright, cheerful outlook and with a love for playing. This will often take the form of a game of "tag" while hanging upside down from the wire of the aviary ceiling. Often they will simply hang upside down for up to half an hour, head twisting up to 360 degrees at times, enthusiastically observing everything that's going on about them.

Because they are a large and relatively active bird they need an aviary of reasonable dimensions. 5 metres (16ft 8in) long will be comfortable for them with a height of at least 2 metres (6ft 8in). It is true that many Kings are kept in smaller aviaries, but in the long run, this is generally to their detriment. Space is needed for them to demonstrate adequately their flying abilities. If they do not have enough room to do this, their flight is very awkward and cumbersome. Confining them to cramped quarters may very quickly bring about stress related death.

Although normally a very hardy species when settled, if only recently purchased or moved, they may show signs of stress, quickly becoming sluggish and losing the desire to eat. If they do eat while in this condition, the goodness in their food is not always adequately utilised as it is excreted in the almost liquid droppings. The birds may soon lose weight and consequently die.

If you are contemplating the purchase of these magnificent looking birds or for some reason have to move them some distance, because they readily suffer stress, there are a few things that one can keep in mind that may help to avoid the heartache of watching them go speedily downhill. When transporting King Parrots don't be alarmed by their continual desperate sounding cries as all Kings have this annoying habit. Although they will mix quite well with some other species, for now, until they have settled, put them into a flight on their own. Someone once described stress as: "any distress or a mental and emotional influence which disrupts normal biological functioning." To be able to maintain that "normal biological functioning" you can offer them foods that contain high levels of vitamin C and pantothenic acid. During periods of stress the bird's needs for ascorbic acid (vitamin C) shoots up sharply. Providing this vitamin at this time it will no doubt be of great value to the birds. For normal maintenance and breeding of birds, ascorbic acid is not required and offering as a supplement will be of no benefit at all, only wasteful. Keep in mind also that vitamin C is the most easily destroyed vitamin of all, by exposure, cooking etc., therefore make sure that fresh supplements are given often whether it be in the form of fruit and vegetables or vitamin powders or liquids.

Pantothenic acid is also vital for any bird undergoing stress, King Parrots though seem particularly prone. Stress actually increases the need for this vitamin. It is needed by all energy-requiring processes within the body. Low intakes of pantothenic acid will mean a slowing down of the bird's metabolic recesses with general harm to the health of it's cells, particularly in the liver, adrenal glands, kidneys, brain and heart, all metabolically active organs. A varied diet and vitamin supplement as outlined in the chapter on Nutritional Requirements will ensure this B complex vitamin is not deficient.

King Parrots are not heavy chewers so can be housed in safety in an aviary constructed of hardwood and a lighter gauge wire and as long as these quarters have space they will not get bored. They have a natural love for trees, in the wild they rarely leave their dense forest habitat. Therefore providing them with fresh gum branches a couple of times each week will go a long way to keeping them happy. As mentioned earlier they are quite happy to mix with other non aggressive species, thus will make excellent neighbours for most other parrots. Cooler climates are favoured by these birds, as their natural habitat depicts, the higher the hills and mountains are, the more abundant they become. They are robust birds in even the most icy weather and the sight of a snow laden tree, decorated with these majestic and fiery looking creatures is indeed a wonderful sight.

In aviaries though, care has to be taken not to allow them to succumb to the problems of chills caused through cold drafts.

Breeding

There are three main obstacles to the successful breeding of King Parrots. Firstly, because some of these parrots have been taken, illegally, from the wild, they are very nervous. If they do survive, it may be a long time before they even settle down enough not to go beserk when their attendant services them, let alone accept a partner for breeding. King Parrots are a relatively inexpensive bird to buy, because many are trapped. If we had to pay the valid price for genuine aviary bred birds, it would unquestionably be many times the price we now pay. To illustrate this point, consider the beautiful 'Sun Conure, although a free breeder they sell for many thousands of dollars, yet our King, which is a recognised difficult breeder is sold, at least in Sydney, for well under two hundred dollars per pair. We must be responsible aviculturists and purchase only those birds that we can reasonably ascertain to be aviary bred stock.

Knowingly buying wild caught birds is unfair on the true breeder as well as adding to the depletion of what one day may be, if trapping continues, a rare species.

The second difficulty to overcome is incompatibility. As a rule, female Kings are dominant and are very particular about their mates. Ideally, when starting with Kings, it is perhaps the best choice to buy young birds, at about six or seven months of age.

By then they are fairly readily sexed and pairs can be set up one per aviary well before they are sexually mature. Obtaining older birds from an unknown source may just mean you are getting someone else's problems. They may not breed, if they do they may be nest deserters, feather pluckers or egg eaters etc. Young hens can be very eager to breed, even when only a year old. Cocks though, are rarely able to fertilise eggs until they are in their third year.

The next barrier to their going down and raising a family is the selection of a log or box in which to do so. Like choosing her husband she is also extremely fussy about her nest. I have found it quicker to establish them as breeders when I have initially offered them more than one log. Their requirements are much the same as their very close relative the Crimson-winged Parrot *Aprosmictus erythropterus*. It is also similar to their brothers and sisters in the wild, preferring a very deep nesting hole, reportedly to a depth of 25m (84ft). Therefore, provide a very deep log or grandfather type box to a depth of at least 1.5 (5ft) or 2m (6ft 8in), sitting it either on or in the ground. The internal diameter needs to be around 25 to 30cm (10-12in). If the log is slightly angled it will not only aid the parents in their comings and goings but may even prevent them from damaging the eggs by jumping on them. Some breeders sit the log into a barrel of soil and try to keep it damp. This will help keep up the required humidity. The only drawback that I have found with natural logs that are so long is that it is very difficult to cut an inspection hole near the base, as logs of this size are normally quite thick. However, a chainsaw seems to be able to manage the job, albeit very rough. If no inspection hole is cut, it can be most difficult finding out what's going on in there. With the top of the log near the roof of the shelter it is impossible to look down into its bowels.

Page 61

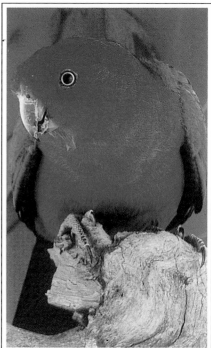

1 - Cock Australian King Parrot.
2 - Australian King Parrots are full bodied with broad, long tails.
3 - Adult cocks clearly display a green wing flash but most hens have little or no flashing.
4 - Hen Australian Kings are easily recognised by the absence of red on their face, head and throat and their black beak.

1 - The single chick from Amboina King father and Eastern King mother at about 5 weeks old.
2 - Cock Amboina King Parrot.
3 - The Cinnamon mutation of the King Parrot.
4 - Adult male Red-wing/King Parrot Hybrid.
5 - The impressive Yellow mutation of the King Parrot.
6 - A hen King Parrot on top of her 6ft high nesting log.

A bit of juggling with a mirror and torch soon has the problem solved, but if the chicks need removing for any reason, the base of the log will have to be removed, causing a great disturbance not to mention physical pain to the keeper.

If she does approve of the nest she will then begin to solicit feeding from her mate. This is done by sitting low on the perch and slightly moving her lowered head up and down in a bobbing motion uttering a low piping sound. He all the while is resplendent as he erects his head feathers, holds his body plumage tight and displays his flash of light green on his wings and dilates the pupils of his eyes. Curiously, on occasions he will stop all this displaying just to have a good old scratch of his head! Hen King Parrots sometimes ignore the nesting receptacles provided for them and drop eggs from the perch or lay them on the ground. One solution that has proved successful when confronted with this problem is to place an open cardboard box on the ground in a quiet, sheltered area. Any salvaged eggs should be placed in the box on the usual nesting material. Some hens have laid more eggs and successfully reared young in this simple situation. It does sound ridiculous but it should be tried. It is surprising how often the simplest solution is the best.

The usual clutch is comprised of about five eggs which the hen alone incubates. In about twenty days the chicks will emerge from the eggs in a thick white down. They fledge at about six or seven weeks and are independent in a further two weeks. Youngsters can be left with their parents without any fear of harm from them.

Occasionally they will double brood, but interestingly in this last season (89/90) a pair in my collection firstly went to nest and produced just one chick, this was taken for hand raising. Very soon after, she commenced nesting again and produced three healthy young, of which I took one for hand raising and left her the remaining two to raise up herself. These two birds fledged near the end of November. After this both adult birds went into a moult. Now, at the time of writing (late March) she is sitting again and has been for just over two weeks. This is her third nesting in one season.

Mutations

The first two Yellow Kings were bred in Germany in 1971, reportedly from two different pairs. And, coincidentally another two yellows from separate pairs in Denmark in 1975. Yellow King Parrots are also becoming established in Australia now. This mutation occurs naturally in the wild here in Australia. There have been some birds bred with "iridescent" green wings but it remains to be seen whether they are significantly different or will become established as a type. A Cinnamon King Parrot too exists in Australian aviaries.

Hybrids

The Australian King has hybridised with Crimson-wings *Aprosmictus erythropterus*, Superbs *Polytelis swainsonii*, Green-winged Kings *Alisterus chloropterus* and with the Amboinan King *Alisterus amboinensis*, this was achieved in my own aviaries with an Amboinan cock and an Australian King hen. In late 1989 they had a clutch of six eggs that produced just one chick followed by a second clutch that produced three young.

Red-capped Parrot

Purpureicephalus spurius

Other Names: *Pileated Parrot, Western King, Hookbill.*

Male

Forehead, crown and nape ruby red; cheeks lime green becoming yellower on the sides of the neck; back, scapulars and upper wing coverts green; breast and abdomen deep violet-purple; vent greenish-yellow tipped with red; thighs red; primary coverts, primaries and under-wing coverts blue; rump and upper tail coverts greenish-yellow; under tail coverts red; central tail feathers green becoming pale blue at the tips; bill pale bluish-grey.

Female

Although adult females are similar in general colouration, the intensity can vary quite considerably. Some are almost as brilliant as males while others are very much duller. She carries more green on the flanks, under the tail and through the red cap of the head.

Sexing

Some birds can be difficult to sex but as a general guide, apart from being duller, the violet purple colour on the chest and abdomen is more violet-grey in females. Hens also have smaller more rounded heads and have a stripe, that is actually formed by a row of white spots, on the underside of each wing.

Immature birds are near impossible to sex with males and females carrying the underwing stripe. Sometimes barely discernible, a young male's head can be flatter and wider.

General

If one were to give a ten year old a palette of brightly coloured paints and ask the child to illustrate a colourful parrot, quite likely the Red-capped Parrot is just what the outcome would look like. Truly, it must be considered one of the most beautiful parrots that grace this Island continent of Australia. Of it, Hutchins and Lovell said in Australian Parrots A Field and Aviary study., "The vivid distinctions in general plumage makes you feel as though you are describing a rainbow; with tints and variations of most colours present, the only colour of the spectrum not included is orange." A description I fully concur with.

In other parts of the world the Red-cap is considered rare, in Australia, each year, hundreds, if not, thousands become available in bird shops, particularly in the East, due to the legal trapping in Western Australia. Even though these thousands of birds are distributed amongst bird keepers and aviculturists each year, there are, relatively few actually held and bred successfully. This often seems to be the case with birds, parrots in particular that are so freely available; they usually never become popular with those that have the ability to care for them properly and breed them, they, being far too common. This really needs to be redressed as it is a certainty that this beautiful parrot will eventually be prevented from being trapped and exported to other states. Even so, in the tiny pocket of south-west Western Australia from whence they come, they are also mercilessly exterminated by the orchardists, who are granted permission to do so by the authorities as the birds are considered vermin. Their unusually shaped bill is designed to open the various native and introduced nuts and fruits from the trees that abound in their natural habitat, particularly the Marri gum Eucalyptus callophylla, Hakea, Dryandra, Banksia and Casuarina. But in spite of their love of these food trees, including their blossoms, every November and December when the orchardist's apples ripen, they are raided by adults and young, who are by now on the wing, alike.

Another reason for them not being so popular is that Red-capped Parrots are extraordinarily flighty. This trait is rarely overcome in trapped birds and their shy nature is even evident in aviary bred specimens. Hand reared birds though, are abundantly at ease by comparison. To house them and make them feel at home and less nervous they should be placed in a large aviary that has a long flight. The more room they have to expend their

1 - KEVIN WILSON

1 - Cock Red-capped Parrot.
2 - Hen Red-capped Parrot.

2 - KEVIN WILSON

1 - Hen Red-cap.
2 - Pair of Red-caps.
Cock on right.
3 - Cock Red-cap.
4 - Hen Red-cap.

nervous energy, until they hopefully settle down, the better for them. As they are so shy I recommend that they be given an area of complete privacy, an area where even their keeper will not intrude. This can be achieved in several ways. Half of the sheltered area can be closed off vertically with a sheet of fibreboard or brushwood fencing. The parrots will quickly recognise the obstacle and soon "hide" around the corner where they will feel safe and comfortable. Another idea is to have the shelter and its perches raised higher than the actual flight, this higher area being opaque to anything on the outside. If an aviary is being adapted, then a horizontal board that is about 50cm (1ft 8in) deep can be fixed to the sheltered area at its entrance, spanning the full width of the flight. The occupants will soon realise the privacy afforded by swooping under the panel and up onto the perch in their hideaway.

Soon the enchanting ways of these birds will shine through and anybody that owns "settled" or tame birds will tell you they are a delight to own. In the book Parakeets, a Handbook to the Imported Species, (1926) a certain Dr Greene is quoted, giving an amusing insight into the character of a tame bird:- "When it perceives anything on the table that it fancies it comes close up to the wires, stretches out its head, and raising its tail to the level of its back, flaps its wings quickly, without, however, opening them out, and emits a series of little calls that sound something like 'chee chu chu' rapidly repeated, but so far, although it answers to its name, 'Pilate,' by the above described call, it has never attempted to speak, or even to imitate any kind of domestic noise, as most of its congeners are in the habit of doing. It is amazingly fond of whittling, and if not supplied with a log of soft wood on which to exercise its long and sharp upper mandible, soon cuts a perch to pieces, or picks holes in the wall; in default of other material it will even nibble the bars of its cage, but it is always supplied with timber, which it converts into minute chips in a very short space of time. Eating little, and always, or nearly always, dry food, it is a very clean bird, bathes frequently, and takes great care of its beautiful plumage, which is in as perfect a condition as if it enjoyed entire liberty, which it might do but for one objection, namely, the havoc it makes of wood of every description picture frames, backs of chairs, and especially the top of an over-mantel, of which it seems to be particularly fond; it has quite a passion for overhauling a desk or box, lifting up the covers of the little receptacles for pens, etc., and pulling out and scattering the contents on all sides. Pencils and penholders it seems to have an extreme liking for and will even try to pull them from one's fingers, when they are speedily broken, or cut rather, into pieces, if the bird is allowed to have its way." I have never known Red-caps to tamper with the wire, but the wood may be a different story. When they have settled in and gained a little confidence,some of them will attack any wooden structures and perches. Others demonstrate not the least bit of interest in chewing and are model inmates in this regard. If all metal aviaries are used to house Red-caps, then either blocks of wood or, preferably, plenty of gum branches should be provided for their powerful beaks to work on.

Red-capped Parrots are keen bathers, even during the coolest of weather,in the other extreme, the hen's bathing habits extend to taking dips and then, soaking wet, enter the nesting box. Even newly fledged young are not reticent about taking the plunge.

Care must be taken in this instance though, that young birds do not go to roost in a soaked state, less there be a cold change at night and they become chilled. This could be disastrous. A separate large, but shallow bowl can be provided as they, especially if they have young as well, will soon empty a drinking vessel of its contents while attending to their ablutions.

Breeding

As has already been discussed privacy is very important in settling these birds, all the more so if they are to breed, and particularly so if they are wild caught birds. They are considered difficult to breed. Red-capped Parrots have the ability to commence breeding when only one year old and are more likely to do so if given a selection of either logs or boxes to choose from. Well before October, the beginning of their breeding season, logs or boxes about 90 to 100 cm (3-3ft 4in) long and about 20cm (8in) in diameter should be hung in place. These sizes though, are only a guide, as most breeding pairs are diverse in their choice, with some selecting a box twice the size that another pair might.

Nesting material can be saw dust and peatmoss or decayed wood to a depth of approximately 75mm (3in). If there is more bedding than required the hen will soon remove it. The males courts his mate by erecting his crown feathers, partially drooping his wings and spreading his tail and deliberately striding along the perch towards his wife, calling very quietly but distinctly to her. Soon after, mating occurs.

Four or five eggs are usually laid, but these can be as many as seven. The female incubates the eggs alone for about twenty days while being fed by the male. During this time because of their skittish nature she should not be disturbed. Red-cap hens have a reputation for desertion, but, I fear, it may be because of human interference rather than their nature, as they customarily, if left alone, sit tight for the full incubationary period. British breeder, George Smith continues:- "When they hatch, the chicks are typical broad tails with long, white, rather thin down eventually replaced by a darker, grey down that comes with the feather pins and there is the invariable white nape-spot of broad tailed parrots. Their bill, as far as I can detect, look rather as other broad tails; but the parents with their elongated bills appear to have some inefficiency in feeding them as the chicks, from the earliest age, always have much food smeared over their heads...." The chicks are noticeably quiet for the first couple of weeks of their lives, they stay in the nest for about thirty three days before emerging as erratic flying fledglings. Sacking or some other soft material may be hung at each end of the aviary at this time to help prevent any damage to the young by crashing. Some youngsters may take up to six weeks before they are fully weaned.

Mutations

At the time of writing there are no recorded mutations in Red-capped Parrots.

Hybrids

Hybrids have been produced by crossing Red-caps with the Red-rump *Psephotus haematonotus*, Crimson Rosella *Platycercus elegans*, Western Rosella *P. icterotis*, Pale-headed Rosella *P. adscitus* and Eastern Rosella *P. eximius*.

Mallee Ringneck Parrot

Barnardius barnardi

Other Names: *Barnard's Parakeet, Ringneck, Bulla Bulla, Buln Buln.*

Male

Overall body green; forehead bright red; crown brownish; ear coverts blue; narrow yellow band on the hind neck and broad orange-yellow (varying) band across the abdomen; mantle dark greenish-blue; wings green with yellowish-green spreading to the medium wing coverts with the outer primary coverts blue and primaries deep royal blue; central tail feathers green turning dark blue at the tips, lateral feathers edged in white; bill greyish-white; eyes dark brown. General colouration can vary greatly in this species both in the wild and in captivity. In an instance of two young birds bred of similar coloured parents, both chicks were markedly different from them and each other. The main area of differentiation being the yellow-orange-red of the abdomen.
Length: 35cm.

Female

Females are duller than the male and slightly smaller.

Sexing

Adult hens are readily sexed in most cases by their less brilliant colour and often narrower head and bill. Most females also sport an under-wing stripe, as do all immature birds. These young are slightly duller again than the female with their crown and nape being brownish and the mantle and back grey-green. Young cocks and hens can sometimes be determined by the shape and size of their heads; full adult colours are reached between twelve and eighteen months.

General

The beautiful Mallee Ringneck is the nominate race of Australian Ringnecks *Barnardius*. Interestingly, they were given their name by the nephew of Napoleon Bonaparte who in 1854, named them after a noted French naturalist. Prince Bonaparte was himself a famed ornithologist.

Mallee Ringnecks are very popular birds with Australian aviculturists because they are brightly coloured, hardy and, with some encouragement, reasonably easily bred. Their popularity has never waned and they have been sought after since their first recorded breeding in captivity in France in 1884. Newcomers to the art of aviculture often find them irresistible, not only because of those points already mentioned but also because they are an inexpensive parrot to buy. They are considered "secure" in captivity and I certainly hope they stay that way as, in its wild state Mallees may eventually become either rare and endangered or even, possibly extinct. World renowned, Australian ornithologist Joseph Forshaw states that the Mallee Ringneck "....does not seem to be able to stand encroaching settlement. As the mallee and wild open woodland are cleared for grazing or cultivation the parrots gradually retreat. They are still considered to be common

1 - KEVIN WILSON

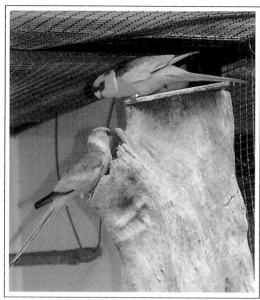

2 - WILSON MOORE

4 - KEVIN WILSON

3 - KEVIN WILSON

1 - Mallee Ringneck hen.
2 - Pair of Mallee
Ringnecks at nesting log.
3 - Mallee Ringneck cock.
4 - Pair of Mallee
Ringnecks. Cock on right.

Page 71

but in some areas do appear to be declining." All members of this race are not unlike Rosellas in their temperament, they can be quite pugnacious and in some instances downright vicious. The large, strong bill of the Mallee is extremely capable of injuring or even killing another bird....through the wire of its aviary. Therefore, wisdom would dictate that Mallees not be housed adjacent to either other members of this race or those equally feisty Rosellas. With more docile Australian or foreign birds, harmony will reign. Hand reared birds too are notoriously aggressive and this is appropriately demonstrated by the late Duke of Bedford, he noted:- "In captivity, or indeed at liberty in this country (England), individual cock Barnards are apt to display the most curious and at times irritating peculiarities of disposition. One very beautiful male in my possession was tame, that is to say he had no fear of humanity. He took but little interest in the society of females of his own race, but devoted his life to the persecution of mankind. For this purpose he stationed himself at the lodge gates and, swooping down upon passers-by, endeavoured to sieze them by the nose!" These birds are active and enjoy plenty of room to fly, 5 metres (16ft 8in) should be deemed the smallest length for them to exercise to the full. Some individuals may get into the habit of chewing wooden structures and those strong beaks are even capable of breaking and unravelling chicken wire, therefore weldmesh or a similar wiring is recommended. Birds in my own possession have shown no interest in bathing either in receptacles provided for that purpose or with open wings in a shower, however, they will sit closed winged, sometimes for hours and seemingly ignorant of the rain that is getting them thoroughly drenched. They spend small amounts of time on the ground foraging for morsals of food, especially if they have been given a fresh supply of seeding grasses and all has been eaten bar that which has fallen to the floor. It is an absolute necessity, therefore, to worm these birds regularly, say, four times annually to keep them free of these death dealing parasites.

Breeding

If space, time and funds allow, several young Mallee Ringnecks can be purchased and housed together. When birds have paired themselves, they can be removed to separate aviaries. By doing this you will alleviate any problems that might occur through your own selection of a pair and the two birds being incompatible. Mature birds especially, if drafted together and take a disliking to each other, may literally knock the stuffing out of one another. So, young birds and patience are advocated when setting up breeding pairs.

Selection of log or box appears to be of paramount importance to these birds, common sense would therefore dictate that a choice of nesting receptacles be offered. In the wild, parrots often have a variety of nesting sites to choose from that not only include height and type of tree but also size and depth of cavity. Serious aviculturists will keep this fundament in mind when offering captive birds nesting haunts. The standard box I have found, and this is by no means the always accepted box, measures about 60cm (2ft) in length with sides that are about 20cm (8in) apart. My own boxes for these birds are hung vertically, but again may not be acceptable this way with other pairs, some breeders having excellent results from nests that are slightly angled. All boxes however, should have sturdy ladders of wire or wooden slats fixed inside to aid the ascent and descent of the parents, the latter though, may well be chewed out by some nesting pairs.

The breeding season begins in August and goes through to December but breedings have been recorded both before and after these months. Courtship begins with the male displaying to his wife, firstly by excitedly flying to and fro the length of the aviary, sometimes with a noticeable but not unduly loud whistle. The hen is then entertained by the cock dancing from side to side of her with his tail spread (Rosella fashion), shoulders squared and sometimes head bobbing while uttering a distinct chattering sound. The normal clutch of eggs is from four to six and are incubated solely by the hen for twenty one days. When the chicks hatch, they remain in the nest for a further thirty to thirty five days. After fledging they continue to be fed by both parents for a further two weeks. The young birds attain their full adult plumage when approximately twelve to eighteen months old. Mallee Ringnecks will sometimes double brood.

Mutations

The only mutation recorded thus far in captivity is a Blue variety that, in good examples is extremely beautiful. The green being replaced by the blue and the yellow by white. In the wild, a Lutino mutation was observed in 1927 by Lang, who: "...saw a pair of young albinos of this species which a woodcutter had taken from the nest; they were of a pale yellow colour, with pink feet and red eyes."

Hybrids

1 - Mallee Ringneck cock.
2 - Mallee Ringnecks have strong beaks and can be very spiteful. They should not be included in mixed aviaries.

Mallee Ringnecks have hybridised with the Port Lincoln B. zonarius, Twenty-eight *B.z. semitoquatus*, Cloncurry B.macgillivrayi, Eastern Rosella *Platycercus eximius*, Western Rosella P. icterotis, Yellow Rosella *P. flavelous* and the Adelaide Rosella *P. adelaidae*.

1 - KEVIN WILSON

2 - KEVIN WILSON

Cloncurry Parrot

Barnardius macgillivrayi

Other Names: *Ringneck Parrot, Macgillivray's Collared Parakeet, Scrub Parrot.*

Male

Overall body pale bluish-green; cheek patches and sides of throat turquoise blue; edge of wing and under tail turquoise blue; neck ring and broad abdominal band lemon-yellow; rump bluish-green washed with yellow; bill bluish-horn; eyes brown.
Length: 33cm.

Female

Similar to the male except she is a little duller and the head sometimes a little smaller.

Sexing

Cloncurries can be difficult to sex, but the size of the head and beak are probably the best guide. The head of the male is wider and flatter than the female's and his beak is marginally larger.

Immature birds are duller versions of their parents except for a distinctive orange frontal band which moults out at about twelve months of age, the first moult.

General

The beautiful Cloncurry Parrot is a sub-species of the Mallee Ringneck *Barnardius barnardi* and its housing and feeding requirements are basically very similar, although it is notably more difficult to breed.

The subtle yet almost iridescent tones of this bird is rarely done justice in descriptive words. Its pleasing colours as well as it being the least belligerent of all the Barnardius family, makes this bird one of the most desirable of Australian parrots.

In the wild it is found in the eastern area of the Northern Territory adjacent to north-western Queensland, wherein lies the town of Cloncurry from whence it got its name.

Housing them presents no real problem, they are though, strong flyers and will take advantage of all the flight space you can offer them. My own birds are housed within flights that are 5 metres (16ft 8in) long and the standard 2 metres (6ft 8in) high and 1 metre (3ft 4in) wide. Consideration must be given to their neighbours if being housed in a complex. They are best not situated along side other Australian Ringnecks or even Rosellas who are also belligerent in their behaviour. The most favourable neighbours would be birds of a more sedate nature such as Princess Parrots *Polytelis alexandrae* or Regents *Polytelis anthopeplus*. They are tough birds that will adapt quite readily to almost any climate but, as are all birds, are intolerant to cold draughts and damp conditions. A shelter properly enclosed on three sides plus a sturdy roof should prevent any problems, especially if it faces a northerly direction where it will allow the warming rays of the winter sun to enter, yet prevent the searing heat of summer from doing so. Some Cloncurries will chew wooden aviary frames while others take no notice of them at all.

Covering frames with either fine wire or sheet metal should solve any problems but this often makes the aviaries less aesthetic. I have found that these birds only chew the wood (and the wire sometimes) when they are bored. This I have overcome by diligently providing them with big, leafy Eucalypt branches, which immediately on being presented with, they clamber into and begin nibbling. It keeps them occupied for hours and I have found that just moving the branch around, if unable to replace, renews their interest.

The Cloncurry's status in aviculture can only be considered as low and therefore they demand a correspondingly higher price than their more readily available brothers in the Barnardius genus. This situation should be remedied before their numbers become any lower, particularly so as they are such easy to keep parrots as well as being one of the most beautiful avian subjects.

Breeding

Cloncurries are not always the easiest birds to induce to breed, they have in my experience often proven difficult to pair up when adult and then, even when this has been achieved, prove to be just as choosey about their nesting facility. A young pair that has been raised together should confirm their compatibility at maturity. Housed as a single pair without the distractions of quarrelsome neighbours, a compatible pair should breed quite readily. They should be offered a choice of at least two nest sites, preferably three, either man-made nest boxes or natural logs. An ideal length would be around 70 to 80cm (2ft 4 in - 2ft 8in) long with an internal diameter of about 15 to 20cm (6 - 8in). Although Cloncurries have accepted boxes and logs without, I have found my best results are obtained with boxes that have a spout protruding from the entrance hole. These boxes are hung vertically in my own aviaries but other aviculturists have had good results also from hanging them on a 45 degree angle.

As the breeding season approaches, usually from about August to December, (Interestingly, I have one pair that bred continually for eighteen months) courtship begins. Much flying to and fro the length of the aviary is carried out while giving short bursts, in succession, of a high pitched whistle. While perching beside the female the male will crouch, square his shoulders, spread his tail and waggle it from side to side, all this accompanied by a soft chattering. Between two to five eggs are laid and incubated by the hen alone for twenty two days. When hatched, the young stay in the nest for a further thirty five days and after fledging are independent in about another two weeks.

This last breeding season afforded me the opportunity to hand raise some Cloncurry chicks. They were taken from the nest when about twelve days old and were subsequently ideal hand raising subjects, pumping at the food with great eagerness from the very first feed. However, as they grew and approached weaning age they became increasingly aggressive, demanding their food and then biting the hand that fed them just for the hell of it.

Once fledged, they would only allow themselves to be handled, even picked up on a finger, when they wanted to be, which was increasingly less and less. This would indicate that these birds would not make good pets, but because they are remarkably steady and quite fearless, would make ideal breeders.

Cloncurries have successfully nested in their first year but it is by far more common for them to do so in their second year.

Some pairs are double brooded. This I have noted depends, to some degree on the weather conditions, if there is plenty of rain, the chances of them going to nest a second time is increased, in dry weather and droughts they may not nest at all.

Mutations

There have been no mutations recorded to date.

Hybrids

The Cloncurry Parrot has hybridised with Mallee Ringneck.

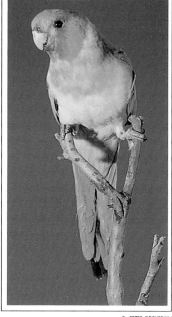

1 - WILSON MOORE

2 - PETER ODEKERKIN

1 - Pair of Cloncurries. Cock on right.
2 - Cock Cloncurry Parrot.
3 - Pair of Cloncurry Parrots. Cock on left.

3 - KEVIN WILSON

1 - CURRUMBIN SANCTUARY

5 - CURRUMBIN SANCTUARY

4 - CURRUMBIN SANCTUARY

2 - IAN BROWN

1 - A 2 day old
Cloncurry chick.
2 - Cock Cloncurry.
3 - Cloncurries love to
fossick around on the
ground.
4 - From left,
Cloncurry chicks 29
and 31 days old.
5 - Cloncurry chicks,
from left 16 and 18
days old.

3 - WILSON MOORE

Page 77

Port Lincoln and Twenty-eight Parrot

Barnardius zonarius & B.z semitorquatus

The Port Lincoln Parrot is the nominate race of these two very similar Australian Ringnecks. The Twenty-eight being a sub-species and aviculturally, differing only in size and colouration. In captivity their housing, feeding and breeding requirements are identical and are therefore covered in the same chapter.

Other Names: *(Port Lincoln) Port Lincoln Ringneck, Yellow-naped Parrot, Yellow-banded Parrot, Bauer's Parakeet.*
(Twenty-eight) Yellow-naped Parrot, Yellow-collared Parrot.

Male

Port Lincoln - Head black; cheeks blue; broad yellow collar on the nape; upper chest green; lower chest distinctly banded with lemon yellow; primary coverts and outer webs of primaries blue; central tail feathers green; outer tail feathers blue tipped with whitish-blue; bill greyish-horn.
Length: 33cm.

Female

Females are similar but slightly duller and smaller.

Male

Twenty-eight - Apart from being a larger bird than the Port Lincoln, the Twenty- eight has two other visually distinguishing features, firstly, a red frontal band above the cere and secondly, a light green abdomen that merges less indistinguishably with the darker green of the chest.
Length: 40cm.

Female

Similar but sometimes slightly smaller and duller.

Sexing

Individual birds can appear very similar in size and colouration. Adult birds are more readily sexed by the male's larger, squarish shaped head, often quite flat on top and a larger and broader bill. Mature females sport a pale white under-wing stripe, but this sometimes disappears as she gets on in years. Apart from the not always discernable shape of the head and the larger bill of males, youngsters are more difficult to sex. Both have the under-wing stripe.

General

Both the Port Lincoln and the Twenty-eight Parrots are striking and make admirable avian subjects. When in peak condition they look immaculate with their shining black heads and contrasting green or yellow bodies. They are lively birds with chatter and whistling (often mimicry) that enchants. Because they are largish parrots and very strong flyers, they require an aviary of at least 5 or 6m (16t 2in - 20ft) long and a metre wide. The height should be no less than 2m (6ft 8in). They also possess beaks that are large and have been known to demolish a timber aviary and wire of a light gauge. Construction therefore, needs to be of metal or of wood covered in galvanised metal sheeting with mesh of a suitable thickness also (minimum 16 gauge). Generally speaking, both species are forest dwellers, where, in the wild they will flit, in small parties, from tree to tree nibbling on leaf tips and buds as well as grubs and nectar from flowering Eucalypts. Branches placed in the aviary for them, fresh each week, will be hungrily chewed to pieces giving them not only nourishment but also "something to do", preventing boredom. Even though they are extremely tough birds, they need adequate protection from damp quarters and inclement weather. Aviaries with solid, wind protecting shelters should be provided. Both species forage from the ground a great deal, so thoughtful consideration needs to be given to the type of flooring, as intestinal worms can easily be picked up, leading to untimely deaths. They will do better in this regard on either a concrete floor or a "stones" floor. That is where the floor of the aviary is covered to a depth of about 25 to 30cm (10 - 12in) with smooth, round or oval stones approximately 25 to 50mm (1 - 2in) in size. This surface is very easily hosed with water and any waste material washed down under the surface where it breaks down naturally and harmlessly. The benefits of such a covering is that it keeps the ground relatively parasite and vermin free, mice and rats being unable to push through this thick layer of heavy stones. The only drawback is where seed is continually dropped in the same area, after a while it clogs up between the stones and begins to grow. This in itself is not a bad thing until it gets too much and eventually becomes sour. The solution is to have a small, square concrete block under the seed bowl or hopper, that can easily be cleaned. All Australian Ringnecks, including the Mallee Ringneck *B. barnardi* and the Cloncurry *B. macgillivrayii*, can be very quarrelsome and aggressive, consequently should never be housed together or aside one another. The same goes for all Rosellas as these too appear to upset them when housed as immediate neighbours.

Breeding

In Australia, neither the Port Lincoln nor the Twenty-eight Parrot are bred in any great numbers. Serious aviculturists need to give some considerable thought to this regrettable situation. Each year thousands of these birds are trapped in Western Australia for the bird trade in the east. They are plentiful and inexpensive, often purchased by the novice bird keeper either for a show aviary (mixed collection) or in an effort to breed them, surmising that they must procreate readily, hence the cheap price. As they are trapped birds, and often cared for in a negligent manner they are undoubtedly under a great deal of stress. Sadly, there are relatively few being bred in captivity and those that are, by novice aviculturists. Without question, sooner or later there will be an end put to the trapping of these birds, we will then have to rely on only aviary bred stock for our supplies and this, as stated, is pitifully low. Demand will increase and prices will obviously escalate. These birds are currently not only being trapped, but are also being slaughtered countlessly by farmers in an effort to defend their valuable crops. Though they appear to be maintaining themselves in the wild, this may not always be. We have a very precarious ecology in this country that has quickly seen the demise of more than one species of bird. Progeny therefore, need to be built up as the foundation of future captive stocks.

Preference should be given to a natural log for these birds over a man-made box, because of their inclination to chew. Not too many boxes possess the durability required by the relentless bill of a persistent female Port Lincoln Parrot. Natural logs are more rugged and more likely to be accepted by birds that have come from the wild. Even though I have never experienced it myself these birds have been known to break their eggs when given a

1 - PETER ODEKERKIN

2 - PETER ODEKERKIN

1 - Cock Port Lincoln.
2 - Pair of Port Lincolns. Cock on right.
3 - Port Lincoln chick 24 days old.

3 - PETER ODEKERKIN

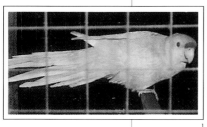

1

5

1 - The red eyed Lutino
mutation of the Twenty-
eight.
2 - Pair of Twenty-eight
Parrots. Cock on left.
3 - Cock Twenty-eight.
4 - Black, blue, green,
yellow and red all blend
well together on the
Twenty-eight Parrot.
5 - The blue mutation
of the Twenty-eight.

nest that is either too deep (more than 70cm. (2ft 4in) in length) or not on an angle. The hen, evidently, rather than hanging on and descending carefully and slowly, drops straight down onto the eggs, destroying them in the process. A shallower log, about 60cm (2ft) long and with an interior diameter of about 15-20cm (6-8in) seems ideal, even more so if slightly angled, enabling the hen to climb down to the chamber with ease. I use a mixture of 50% sawdust and shavings with 50% peatmoss as bedding. I have often found partially chewed gum leaves in the nest too, this may indicate the importance of making available to them supplies of fresh gum branches with their leaves as often as possible.

Courtship is not unlike that of Rosellas, with the male head-bobbing and bowing before the female. He squares his shoulders, raises his wings slightly and fans his tail while chattering and twittering his special courtship note to her. Between four and seven eggs may be laid with incubation beginning with the laying of the second or third egg. Four eggs comprise the normal clutch with incubation lasting about twenty one days. The hen alone incubates, but is fed to some extent by the male.

Usually early mornings and late afternoons finds her emerging from the nest to feed herself. He will also sometimes aid in the feeding of the young, but this is not always tolerated by the hen. The young are in the nest for approximately thirty eight days before fledging and are independent in a further two weeks. Immature birds reach the full depth of their hand some plumage at about fourteen or fifteen months of age. They are sometimes double brooded.

In the wild there is considerable overlap in the range of these two birds, consequently there is a vast amount of hybridisation. Often one sees more hybrids for sale in bird shops than the true species. We should, nevertheless, endeavour to purchase and breed only those birds that exhibit colours true to their type, keeping them as pure as possible.

Mutations

The late Duke of Bedford was the first to report a Blue mutation of the Port Lincoln in the United Kingdom, although this particular bird never produced young. There are now a very few Blue birds in Australian aviaries.

Twenty-eights. In 1974, an Australian aviculturist had what might be termed as "beginners luck", the first Twenty-eight Parrot that he had ever reared was a Yellow one. In 1926, Perth zoo had a single Blue mutation on display, since then a few more have popped up here and there. Even rarer in Australia is the Lutino Twenty-eight. Both the Blue and Lutino mutation of the Twenty-eight Parrot have been recorded in the wild.

Hybrids

In the wild there is considerable overlap in the range of these two birds, consequently there is a vast amount of hybridisation. Often one sees more hybrids for sale in bird shops than the true species. We should, nevertheless, endeavour to purchase and breed only those birds that exhibit colours true to their type, keeping them as pure as possible.

Port Lincolns have otherwise hybridised with Mallee Ringnecks *Barnardius barnardi*, Superbs *Polytelis swainsonii*, Pale-headed Rosellas *Platycercus adscitus* and Crimson Rosellas *Platycercus elegans*.

Kakariki Parrot

Cyanoromphus

Red-fronted Kakariki *C. novaezelandiae*

Other Names: *Red-fronted Parakeet, Red-crowned Parrot, Red-headed Parrot.*

Male

Body overall deep green; forehead and crown crimson red with a red patch behind each eye; a patch of crimson on either side of the rump; primaries and outer primaries rich dark blue; bill light metallic grey with a blacktip; eyes red.
Length: 28cm.

Female

Identical colouration but slightly smaller in size.

Yellow-fronted Kakariki *C. auriceps*

Other Names: *Yellow-fronted Parakeet, Yellow-crowned Parrot, Yellow-headed Parrot.*

Male

As described for the Red-fronted but the crown being golden yellow and a red band above the cere. They also lack any trace of red behind the eye.
Length: 25cm.

Female

Females have the same colouration but are smaller.

Sexing

A single bird can sometimes be extremely difficult to sex, particularly if the individual happens to be a rather larger or smaller specimen than the norm. If however, you have two birds, one of each sex, the difference in the size and broadness of the bill is clearly seen, the male having the larger and broader bill. When the bill size appears indistinguishable between two birds it will be most likely they are the same sex. Immature Kakarikis display a duller red or yellow cap than their parents and have shorter tails, but can still be sexed readily as above.

General

Kakarikis are obviously not Australian parrots at all but hale from our closest neighbour, New Zealand. Australian aviculture though, has played such an important role in the preservation of these remarkable little birds in their natural habitat, I felt they should be included in this book. They are now in great numbers in aviaries throughout Australia and the numbers of the above two races are increasing in the wild. Not too long ago when the Red-fronted Kakariki was in danger of becoming extinct both in the wild and New Zealand aviaries, in fact there were only 103 officially held in captivity in New Zealand in 1958, they were eventually in the early seventies, collected by the authorities from Australian aviculturists for release into their native habitat. Although the Red-fronted Kakariki is still under threat in the wild, stocks of them, not only in Australia but world wide will hopefully ensure that extinction, at least for this little parrot, will never occur.

In the aviary these birds are quite unique, unlike many parrots they do not have loud raucous calls or whistles, but very gentle and quiet chattering sounds and sometimes musical notes, which if you live in a city or built up area is a decided blessing as only the most disagreeable of neighbours could ever complain. Their other attributes also make them highly desirable avian subjects. They are not nervous birds that throw themselves into a panic as you approach the aviary, but inquisitive birds that will soon be hopping within centimetres of you when you enter their aviary. Eating from your hand becomes a regular daily pleasure that they eagerly await. One couldn't be blamed for even thinking that they enjoy being in human company. Kakarikis are extremely active birds and watching their amazing antics is positively delightful. They have the ability to fly very swiftly, performing aerobatics in sometimes very confined spaces. I have seen most parrots run up the wire before and even some, with the aid of their beak, run down, but these are the only birds I have seen running down the wire using only their two, long feet! They seem to make a thorough game of this, playfully climbing and exploring every centimetre of their aviary. The floor too is not neglected, with their long, chicken like legs they scratch and dig in the soil for a tid-bit of food like a dropped piece of fruit or an escaping insect. It may be interesting to note at this juncture that, one pair of my Yellow-fronteds have never taken dry seed. They prefer to eat entirely fruit and vegetable matter with only a little soaked seed.

A dirt floor will be thoroughly enjoyed by Kakarikis and to make it a little more enjoyable for them, leaf litter should be gathered and spread thickly over the floor. If you have concrete floors to your aviaries, then this addition will be appreciated all

1 - KEVIN WILSON

2 - KEVIN WILSON

1 - Red-fronted
Kakariki cock.
2 - Pied Red-fronted
Kakariki

1 - KEVIN WILSON

2 - WILSON MOORE

5 - KEVIN WILSON

3 - KEVIN WILSON

4 - KEVIN WILSON

1 - Pied mutation of
the Red-fronted
Kakariki.
2 - Kakarikis like this
Red-fronted always
have that inquisitive
look.
3 - Yellow-fronted
Kakariki.
4 - Yellow-fronted
Kakariki cock.
5 - Yellow-fronted
Kakariki hen.

the more because as they scratch around in it they will disturb many of the little bugs and other creatures that reside amongst it, chasing them and eating them. If this isn't available, then sods of earth with grass growing from them will be most agreeable to them, falling upon them the very instant they are offered. Because they spend so much time on the ground, they are subjected to worm infestation, therefore regular de-worming is a must, ideally four times per year. It has often been reported that Kakarikis "suddenly" die, for no apparent reason, could it be that they are not being wormed adequately or often enough? These birds when fed the correct diet, housed appropriately and regularly wormed will live up to fifteen or sixteen years, even breeding into their twelfth year.

Even though they are a very active bird, a very large aviary for one pair is not really necessary, as I have stated, they do make use of every centimetre of space available to them, obtaining all the exercise they need. However, I suggest an aviary of no smaller than 2.5m (8ft 4in) long, 2m (6ft 8in) high and a metre (3ft 4in) wide. These active and inquisitive birds do not need heavy steel fortresses. Wooden aviaries with even chicken wire will suffice as they are neither destructive to the wooden frames or aviary furnishings. They are, nevertheless, extremely capable escape artists. If there is so much as a torn piece of mesh or a gap between the door and frame, they will find it quickly and be out. In most instances though, it won't be long before they are back, clinging to the wire trying to find their way back in. Because they have little fear of their owners, they can soon be netted and placed back in the safety of their homes. A British aviculturist, Professor J.R. Hodges once said of them: "The Red-fronted Parakeet is a delightful aviary inhabitant. In addition to its beauty and its attractive mannerisms, it is hardy, easy to keep, easy to breed and extremely intelligent. On one occasion, the feeding hatch of the aviary of the adult pair was accidently left open. Within seconds both the male and female were apparently enjoying their newfound freedom and exploring the neighbourhood. After about half an hour's exercise, during which they came off worse in an altercation with the local Blackbirds, they flew back to the garden. They found their aviary with no difficulty, even though it is one in a group of identical compartments, and returned sedately through the feeding hatch." Kakarikis enjoy nibbling on fresh gum leaves especially if they have nuts on them and although they will not chew the wooden components of the aviary, will gnaw at these branches. They also love to bathe, even in the coldest weather, so a shallow bowl of fresh water should always be available for this purpose. Speaking of cold weather, Kakarikis thrive in it, showing no discomfort whatsoever even in the bleakest weather. On the other hand, in hot weather they are extremely uncomfortable. Their aviary then, should be situated in a shady area to keep off the extreme heat of the sun and a garden sprinkler or soaker hose at the ready if needed.

Breeding

Kakarikis are free breeders that take virtually every opportunity to breed when provided with all their basic requisites. They are capable of parenting up to twelve chicks at a time, although it is far more common to have about five. They are further remarkable in their ability to breed when extremely young. On many occasions it has been recorded that hens as young as just five months have successfully raised a family and a cock at only four months fertilising eggs.

I have been keeping and breeding Kakarikis for a number of years now and found that the consistently most successful box to use is a typical, horizontal, African Lovebird nest box, dimensions approximately 15cm (6in) deep x 15cm (6in) high and 30cm (12in) wide. Initially, three boxes are hung in place at a slight angle. Make sure that they are not hung in either the highest or hottest part of the aviary as parents and young may suffer heat induced stress. When a nest is chosen, it may be best to remove the others to prevent the hen laying some eggs in one box and more in another. Peat and sawdust are mixed together and placed in the box to a depth of about 40 or 50mm (1.5-2in) where the hen will lay her eggs in a small depression. Usually the cock will investigate first and then invite the hen into the box, this, sometimes with a peculiar shaking of their heads from left to right and chattering to one another. Incubation, I have sometimes found to be erratic, the normal period of time being twenty days. One note worthy clutch, from the first egg being laid to the last hatching of a nest of six chicks, (seven eggs were laid but one disappeared) was an astonishing thirty six days! By the time the young chicks have their pin feathers coming through it can be very crowded in that box, so I level the box out, giving the young a little more room. When hatched, the chicks are covered in a thick grey down. They leave the nest at about five weeks of age and when the young are independent at about seven or eight weeks they can be removed to another aviary as the hen may well be considering another clutch or may even have already laid.

Kakarikis in good health and condition may breed all year round, even in snow, producing four clutches in twelve months. However, I do not recommend such a heavy breeding programme as not only will it exhaust the hen, but considerably shorten her breeding life, perhaps to only four or five years, where as with consideration for their health and abilities, this can be extended to twice as long, sometimes longer. Two clutches should be quite enough for any pair in one year. Some breeders prevent their birds from breeding during the hottest summer months as some have not only lost chicks but also sitting mothers, expiring from heat exhaustion. Great care needs to be taken not to cross breed Yellow-fronteds with their Red-fronted counterparts. Some thoughtless Australian breeders have done so and then had the gall to sell them as Orange-fronteds. True Orange-fronteds C. malherbi differ from these hybrids by having a paler yellow crown than the Yellow-fronted and being much smaller (20cm/ 8in) in size. There are no true Orange-fronted Kakarikis kept in Australian aviaries to my knowledge.

Mutations

Several yellow birds have been bred both overseas and in Australia but, as yet, are far from being established. Pied Kakarikis are becoming more numerous, showing yellow feathers to varying degrees.

Hybrids

The only known hybrid, apart from that mentioned above is with a Naretha Blue-bonnet *Psephotus haematogaster narethae.*

Publisher's Note

This title is published by Australian Birdkeeper Publishing who produce a wide and varied range of avicultural literature including the world acclaimed Australian Birdkeeper magazine - a full colour, bi-monthly magazine specifically designed for birdlovers and aviculturists. It is the intention of the publishers to produce high quality, informative literature for birdlovers, fanciers and aviculturists alike throughout the world. It is also the publishers' belief that the dissemination of qualified information on the care, keeping and breeding of birds is imperative for the total well-being of captive birds and the increased knowledge of aviculturists.

Nigel Steele-Boyce
Publisher/Editor-In-Chief
Australian Birdkeeper

Quality Publications from Australian Birdkeeper

- A Guide to Asiatic Parrots in Australia.
- A Guide to Basic Health & Disease in Birds.
- A Guide to Cockatiels & their Mutations.
- A Guide to Eclectus Parrots.
- A Guide to Gouldian Finches.
- A Guide to Neophema & Psephotus Grass Parrots.
- A Guide to Australian Long & Broad-tailed Parrots and New Zealand Kakarikis.
- A Guide to Lories & Lorikeets.
- A Guide to Pigeons, Doves & Quail.
- A Guide to Rosellas.

- Anthology of Birdkeeping.

- Australian Birdkeeper Bi-monthly magazine.

For further information and our FREE Catalogue on any of Australian Birdkeeper quality products/publications write to:

Australian Birdkeeper
P.O. Box 6288, South Tweed Heads,
NSW 2486 Australia.
or
Phone: (07) 5590 7777 Fax: (07) 5590 7130
Email: birdkeeper@birdkeeper.com.au
http://www.birdkeeper.com.au

Bibliography
Australian Parrots in Bush and Aviary . . . . Ian Harman
Australian Parrots - a Field and Aviary Study . . . . . . B.R. Hutchins and R.H. Lovell
Hand Rearing Parrots . . . . Rosemary Low
Parrots, Thier Care and Breeding . . . . Rosemary Low
Parrots of the World . . . . Joseph M. Forshaw
Parrakeets, a Handbook to the Imported Species . . . . David Seth-Smith
Lovebirds and Related Parrots. . . . . George A. Smith
Nutrition of Finches and Other Cage Birds . . . . Robert G. Black
Australian Birdkeeper Magazine